Exploring British Culture

Multi-level activities about life in the UK

CAMBRIDGE
UNIVERSITY PRESS

Jo Smith

CAMBRIDGE
UNIVERSITY PRESS

University Printing House, Cambridge CB2 8BS, United Kingdom

Cambridge University Press is part of the University of Cambridge.

It furthers the University's mission by disseminating knowledge in the pursuit of education, learning and research at the highest international levels of excellence.

www.cambridge.org
Information on this title: www.cambridge.org/9780521186421

© Cambridge University Press 2012

First published 2012
Reprinted 2014

Printed in the United Kingdom by Hobbs the Printers Ltd

A catalogue record for this publication is available from the British Library

ISBN 978-0-521-18642-1 Paperback with Audio CD

Contents

Map of the book   4

Introduction   6

Map of the UK   9

Unit 1   The United Kingdom today   10

Unit 2   A look at the United Kingdom   16

Unit 3   People in the UK   22

Unit 4   How the UK is governed   28

Unit 5   Society, family and class   34

Unit 6   Food   40

Unit 7   Money and work   46

Unit 8   Celebrations, beliefs and values   52

Unit 9   British history   58

Unit 10   Health and welfare   64

Unit 11   Leisure time   70

Unit 12   The media and communication   76

Unit 13   Education and learning   82

Unit 14   Creative arts and culture   88

Unit 15   Housing and the local community   94

Unit 16   British legal system   100

Unit 17   Wild Britain   106

Unit 18   21st Century Britain   112

Audioscript   118

Map of the book

Organisation of the units

Theme	Unit	Topic	Type of Activity	Level
1 The United Kingdom today	1.1	In the UK	Listening and matching activity	Elem to Pre-int
	1.2	What do you know about the UK?	Communicative quiz	Intermediate
	1.3	A view of the UK	Listening and information exchange	Advanced
2 A look at the United Kingdom	2.1	British capital cities	Discussion and matching activity	Elem to Pre-int
	2.2	A profile of London	Reading and information gap fill	Intermediate
	2.3	Regions and counties of the UK	Reading and listening for information	Advanced
3 People in the UK	3.1	Who lives in the UK?	Reading and listening activity	Elem to Pre-int
	3.2	British men and women	Listening, information gap fill and discussion	Intermediate
	3.3	Minority groups in Britain	Listening, reading and discussion	Advanced
4 How the UK is governed	4.1	A guide to the British government	Matching activity and Information search	Elem to Pre-int
	4.2	Everyday politics	Reading and information search	Intermediate
	4.3	How the government works	Reading, listening and discussion	Advanced
5 Society, family and class	5.1	The Royal Family	Listening and information search	Elem to Pre-int
	5.2	British families	Reading, listening, gap fill and discussion	Intermediate
	5.3	The British class system	Listening for information and discussion	Advanced
6 Food	6.1	What's on the menu?	Listening and matching activity	Elem to Pre-int
	6.2	The story of British food	Listening for information and discussion	Intermediate
	6.3	21st-century food in Britain	Reading for information and discussion	Advanced
7 Money and work	7.1	The British money system	Reading, listening and information search	Elem to Pre-int
	7.2	The cost of living	Reading comprehension and discussion	Intermediate
	7.3	High finance	Reading for information and discussion	Advanced
8 Celebrations, beliefs and values	8.1	British celebrations	Reading and information exchange	Elem to Pre-int
	8.2	Religious and non-religious festivals	Reading and information exchange	Intermediate
	8.3	Attitudes and values	Reading, gap fill and discussion	Advanced
9 British history	9.1	British history chart	Reading and matching activity	Elem to Pre-int
	9.2	A date with British history	Reading, listening and information search	Intermediate
	9.3	People who changed British history	Listening, information search and debate	Advanced

Theme	Unit	Topic	Type of Activity	Level
10 Health and welfare	**10.1**	The National Health Service	Reading and information search	Elem to Pre-int
	10.2	British charities	Matching activity and discussion	Intermediate
	10.3	The welfare state	Reading gap fill, listening and discussion	Advanced
11 Leisure time	**11.1**	How the British relax	Listening for information and discussion	Elem to Pre-int
	11.2	Some British pastimes	Reading and information exchange	Intermediate
	11.3	Taking time out	Listening for information and discussion	Advanced
12 The media and communication	**12.1**	News in the UK	Reading and information search	Elem to Pre-int
	12.2	In the news	Reading, listening and discussion	Intermediate
	12.3	The BBC	Listening quiz and discussion	Advanced
13 Education and learning	**13.1**	The learning journey	Listening and reading, gap fill	Elem to Pre-int
	13.2	Education in the UK	Reading and matching activity	Intermediate
	13.3	Learning for life	Information exchange and word game	Advanced
14 Creative arts and culture	**14.1**	Local arts and crafts	Reading, information search and discussion	Elem to Pre-int
	14.2	British creative arts	Listening, matching and reading activity	Intermediate
	14.3	British artistic achievement	Reading, listening and discussion	Advanced
15 Housing and the local community	**15.1**	Where people live	Listening and information gathering	Elem to Pre-int
	15.2	Home sweet home	Reading and discussion	Intermediate
	15.3	British housing issues	Reading and discussion	Advanced
16 British legal system	**16.1**	People in the law	Reading and information search	Elem to Pre-int
	16.2	Law in the UK	Reading and discussion	Intermediate
	16.3	Legal concerns	Listening for information and discussion	Advanced
17 Wild Britain	**17.1**	The countryside and the seasons	Listening for information	Elem to Pre-int
	17.2	The town and the countryside	Listening and discussion	Intermediate
	17.3	UK country matters	Reading, gap fill and discussion	Advanced
18 21st Century Britain	**18.1**	Britain and the rest of the world	Reading and matching activity	Elem to Pre-int
	18.2	The journey to the 21st Century	Information exchange and listening	Intermediate
	18.3	Values and visions	Reading and information exchange	Advanced

Introduction

Who is *Exploring British Culture* for?

Exploring British Culture has been written for teachers of EFL, ESL and ESOL and of English for Academic Purposes in schools and colleges throughout the world. It contains photocopiable materials for the classroom which can be used to support British Culture, British Citizenship and General English courses. These activities provide self-contained lessons for the busy teacher aimed at learners undertaking courses from Elementary to Advanced levels.

How is *Exploring British Culture* organised?

The activity book is divided into 18 units, exploring key aspects of life in the UK. Each unit contains three lessons of topic-based material of differing levels. The first is aimed at Elementary to Pre-intermediate learners, the second at Intermediate learners and the third at Advanced learners. For example:

Unit 3: People in the UK
3.1: Who lives in the UK?   (Elementary to Pre-intermediate)
3.2: British men and women   (Intermediate)
3.3: Minority groups in Britain   (Advanced)

The map of the book provides a clear guide to the 18 units and 54 lessons and includes references to activity types, skills practised and level. The audio script is located at the back of the book.

What topics are covered in the units?

The topics have been carefully chosen to reflect key aspects of British culture. They include: the geography of Britain and the structure of British society; the people who live in the UK, their views, attitudes and cultural identities; British government, history, law, finances, education, housing, health and social welfare; British social and cultural activities, beliefs and values; the creative arts and media; 21st Century Britain and its future.

How is each unit organised?

Each unit consists of a lesson on two facing pages with step-by-step teachers' notes on the left side and a photocopiable worksheet on the right side. Each lesson aims to provide around 45–60 minutes of teaching, plus a lesson warmer and an extension activity.

The teachers' notes include:

- **Information panel**
  This describes the type of activity and skills practised, the aims of the unit, the level or levels covered in the unit, a list of vocabulary that may require pre-knowledge or pre-teaching and the preparation required prior to delivery of the lesson.

- **Warmer**
  This aims to get the learners thinking about the theme, introduce or elicit required lexis around the unit topic and prepare learners for the main activity.

- **Teaching procedures**
  These offer clear guidance on the teaching and delivery of the lesson. Some lessons include a choice of delivery options with procedures supporting differentiation within learner groups or classrooms.

- **Extension activity**
  These tasks suggest a range of ways to further develop the theme. They offer skills development in the form of interviews, role-plays, discussion, presentations and debates and other communicative activities. Online research and writing activities are developed in the contexts of British culture books, wall charts, class blogs and videos and radio programmes. Ideas on language and lexis development are offered as well as pronunciation practice, comprehension of register and effective communication techniques.

The worksheets include:

- **Factual information** on aspects of British culture within the unit theme, at the appropriate levels for the groups.
- **Authentic materials** from interviews, articles, books, reports and with information up to date at the time of publishing
- **Instructions** to learners on how to undertake tasks and to teachers when doing cut-out activities.

How will *Exploring British Culture* help students?

These materials offer a unique opportunity for teachers to deliver high quality, relevant and stimulating materials on all aspects of British cultural life to a range of learners within their classrooms. In addition, learners are offered opportunities to reflect on, and express, their views of historic and modern Britain.

Learners are also given the chance to explore their own cultural and social practices and make comparisons with the habits of their everyday lives. It is hoped these activities will encourage greater understanding of the wide range of values, beliefs and concerns held by people in the UK. It will try to identify/explain how British people live their lives and how British society works. We hope you will enjoy using these materials.

Thanks and acknowledgements

I am very grateful to the following individuals who offered valuable help or contributed to the development of the book.

I would like to extend my thanks to Raymond Tinney for his support through the writing process and his advice on the Northern Ireland sections. Thanks also go to Valerie Mainstone for her feedback on the British history and Scottish sections.

I am also very grateful to my colleagues who offered their help and thoughts on the materials and also the many teachers who gave encouragement and advice on the project. In particular, I would like to thank Mary Spencer and her family for their valued contribution and to Susan Kingsley for her interest and support in the project. Thanks also go to Tim Misra and his family and members of the Polish and Iranian communities who have enabled me to draw from their experiences.

Many thanks go to my British family: Linda and Anthony, Sophie and Oliver for their support and feedback throughout the writing process. Thanks also go to Stephanie and Michael Allen, George, Sally, Brigitte and my extended family in Australia, where ideas on culture and identity were initially discussed and the concept of 'Britishness' was first explored.

I would finally like to thank Tom Allen and Helen Forrest for their perceptive comments and excellent editing, and to Frances Disken and Cambridge University Press for giving me the opportunity to research and develop these materials.

Acknowledgements

The authors and publishers acknowledge the following sources of copyright material and are grateful for the permissions granted. While every effort has been made, it has not always been possible to identify the sources of all the material used, or to trace all copyright holders. If any omissions are brought to our notice, we will be happy to include the appropriate acknowledgements on reprinting.

The publisher has used its best endeavours to ensure that the URLs for external websites referred to in this book are correct and active at the time of going to press. However, the publisher has no responsibility for the websites and can make no guarantee that a site will remain live or that the content is or will remain appropriate.

The text and audio on pp. taken from Prime Minister's questions 9/2/11. Contains Parliamentary information licensed under the Open Parliament Licence v1.0.; The quote on p. Lord Birkett (1960) Contains Parliamentary information licensed under the Open Parliament Licence v1.0.; The quote on p.33 Education Service, Contains Parliamentary information licensed under the Open Parliament Licence v1.0.;'The text on p.45 'Let's have a cull of the fast food joints, demands Jamie Oliver' by Jason Beattie, 2008 ©Mirrorpix, Mirror Syndication International.

Illustrations by Kathy Baxendale, Ian@ Kja-Artists, Sandy Nichols, David Shephard.

Photos: p. 11 (CL): Shutterstock/great_photos; p. 11 (CR): Shutterstock/John A Cameron; p. 11 (BL): Shutterstock/Gail Johnson; p. 11 (BR): Shutterstock/Josemaria Toscano; p. 17 (L): Shutterstock/Vitaly Titov & Maria Sidelnikova; p. 17 (CL), 91 (L) and 105 (C): Thinkstock; p. 17 (CR): Shutterstock/Avella; p. 17 (R): Shutterstock/Tim Dobbs; p. 27 (L): Shutterstock/Michael Zysman; p. 27 (R): © mpworks / Alamy; p. 33: Shutterstock/Adam Gregor; p. 37 (L): Shutterstock/Jason Stitt; p. 37 (CL), 39 (C), 43 (CR) and 89 : Thinkstock/Jupiterimages; p. 37 (CR): Thinkstock/Comstock; p. 37 (R): Thinkstock/Creatas; p. 39 (R): Thinkstock/ Dave J. Anthony; p. 39 (L): Shutterstock/Neil Roy Johnson; p. 43 (L): Shutterstock/Monkey Business Images; p. 43 (CL): Shutterstock/erkanupan; p. 43 (R): Shutterstock/Edward Westmacott; p. 45 (R): Shutterstock/Andrei Zarubaika; p. 45 (L): Shutterstock/Elena Rostunova; p. 47: Shutterstock/Guy Erwood; p. 49: © Justin Kase zsixz / Alamy; p. 59 (TL): Shutterstock/ Matthew Jacques; p. 59 (TC): Shutterstock/T. Kimmeskamp; p. 59 (TR): Shutterstock/T. Kimmeskamp; p. 59 (CR): Shutterstock/Cliff Lloyd; p. 59 (C) and 75 (CL): Shutterstock; p. 59 (CL): Shutterstock/Pawel Nawrot; p. 59 (BL): Shutterstock/TTphoto; p. 59 (BC): Shutterstock/ trevorb; p. 59 (BR): Shutterstock/David Burrows; p. 61 (L & CR): © The Trustees of the British Museum; p. 61 (CL): Thinkstock/Photos.com; p. 61 (R): © Michael Foyle / Alamy; p. 65: © Andrew Aitchison / Alamy; p. 75 (TR): Getty Images; p. 75 (CR): Tim Graham/Getty Images; p. 75 (BL): © Andrew Fox/Corbis; p. 75 (BR): © Paul Tomlins/Lebrecht Music & Arts/Corbis; p. 79: Shutterstock/Avella; p. 85 (L): Shutterstock/ChipPix; p. 85 (R): Shutterstock/RTimages; p. 91 (C): Alamy; p. 93 (L & R) and 99 (BC): Getty Images; p. 95 (TL): Shutterstock/haak78; p. 95 (TC): Shutterstock/Mark William Richardson; p. 95 (TR): Shutterstock/Terence Mendoza; p. 95 (BR): Shutterstock/David Hughes; p. 95 (BC): Shutterstock/Gergo Orban; p. 95 (BL): Shutterstock/ronfromyork; p. 99 (T): Shutterstock/r.nagy; p. 99 (UC): Shutterstock/Mark William Richardson; p. 99 (B): © Photofusion Picture Library / Alamy; p. 105 (BC): Shutterstock/Stephen Finn; p. 105 (B): © Marco Secchi / Alamy; p. 105 (T): Shutterstock/ isaxar; p. 105 (UC): Shutterstock/Morphart; p. 109 (L): © Adrian Sherratt / Alamy; p. 109 (R): Thinkstock/Hemera Technologies.

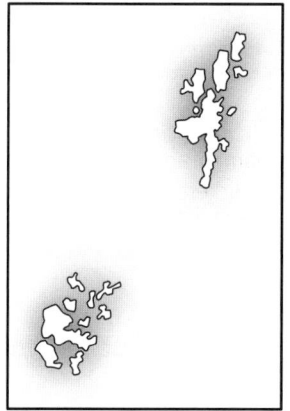

1.1

In the UK

TYPE OF ACTIVITY
Listening and matching activity

LEVEL
Elementary to Pre-intermediate

TIME
40–50 minutes

AIMS
To develop an awareness of well-known British images and symbols

VOCABULARY
cricket, famous, flag, giant, leek, million, rose, shamrock, symbol, thistle, whisky, Britain, England, Scotland, Wales, Northern Ireland, The United Kingdom, Loch Ness monster

PREPARATION
Display a large map of the British Isles. One photocopy of the worksheet for each learner. Take in dictionaries.

Warmer

Ask learners if they have been to the UK. Ask them where they went and what they saw. Focus learners on a large map of the British Isles. Ask them what countries they can see on it. Write their answers on the board and locate the countries on the map. (British Isles: England, Scotland, Wales, Northern Ireland, the Republic of Ireland. The British Isles is the geographical name for all the islands in the group.) Then ask learners what countries are in the United Kingdom. (England, Scotland, Wales and N. Ireland. The Republic of Ireland is not in the UK.) Ask learners if they know any of the capital cities and write these on the board. (London, Edinburgh, Cardiff and Belfast.)

1 Give out one copy of the worksheet to each learner. Focus them on the map. Working in pairs, learners read through the first paragraph. Learners locate the countries of the United Kingdom and write these on the map. Next, learners locate the capital cities and write these on the map. They can go up to the large map to check their work, as appropriate. Go over the answers with the class.

> **Answers**
>
> **a** Scotland **b** Northern Ireland **c** England **d** Wales
> **E** Belfast **F** Edinburgh **G** Cardiff **H** London
> The Welsh flag, with the dragon on it, is not represented on the Union Jack. NB Northern Ireland has not got an official flag. The flag here is *St. Patrick's Saltire*.

2 Focus learners on the British flag on the front of the book. Ask them if they know its name (the Union Jack). Read the sentence about the Union Jack together. Focus learners on the four information boxes. Learners work in pairs and label the four countries, using the visuals as clues. Check the answers with the class. Look at the symbols and ask learners to guess the symbol for each country. (The answers to these are in the audio.)

3 ▶ 2-5 Tell learners they are going to hear some information about each country. Play the audio while learners complete the information boxes. Learners check their answers in pairs. Play the audio again, then go over the answers with the class. Discuss any points arising.

> **Answers**
>
> | | Country | Population | Famous place | Famous for ... |
> | --- | --- | --- | --- | --- |
> | **1** | England | 50 million+ | London Eye | buildings, Shakespeare, cricket |
> | **2** | Scotland | 5 million | Ben Nevis | whisky, the kilt, Nessie (the Loch Ness Monster) |
> | **3** | Northern Ireland | 2 million | Giant's Causeway | pubs, music, dancing |
> | **4** | Wales | 3 million | Conwy castle | mountains, singing, rugby |

4 ▶ 6-7 Focus learners on the pronunciation of the countries, highlighting vowel sounds and the word stress on the first syllables: England /ˈɪŋglənd/; Ireland /ˈaɪələnd/; Wales /weɪlz/; Scotland /ˈskɒtlənd/. Go over the pronunciation of the cities: London /ˈlʌndən/; Cardiff /ˈkɑːdɪf/; Belfast /ˈbelfɑːst/; Edinburgh /ˈedɪnbʌrʌ/. (The e in England and English is pronounced /ɪ/ as in ship, not /e/ as in help.) Also practise the semi-vowels: /w/ and /j/, e.g. Wales /weɪlz/. (Semi-vowels are consonants but, like vowels, the lips do not meet when pronounced.) Play the audio to practise the pronunciation. Tell learners that the noun and adjective forms need capitals when written.

Extension

Learners write a book/blog about the UK. They can use the pictures and information from this activity to plan, and put together, their own pages about each country. They can also bring in other pictures and short texts about the buildings or places that interest them. Learners can continue to develop a British culture book in subsequent lessons. A wall chart with key information and facts can also be developed by the learners.

1 There are four countries in the United Kingdom. These are England, Scotland, Wales and Northern Ireland. The names of the capital cities are Edinburgh, Cardiff, Belfast and London.

1 Look at the map on the right. Can you write the names of the countries on the map? (a–d)

2 Can you write the names of the capital cities on the map? (E–H)

3 The flag of the United Kingdom is called the Union Jack. The flag of one country is not in the Union Jack. What country is it? ....

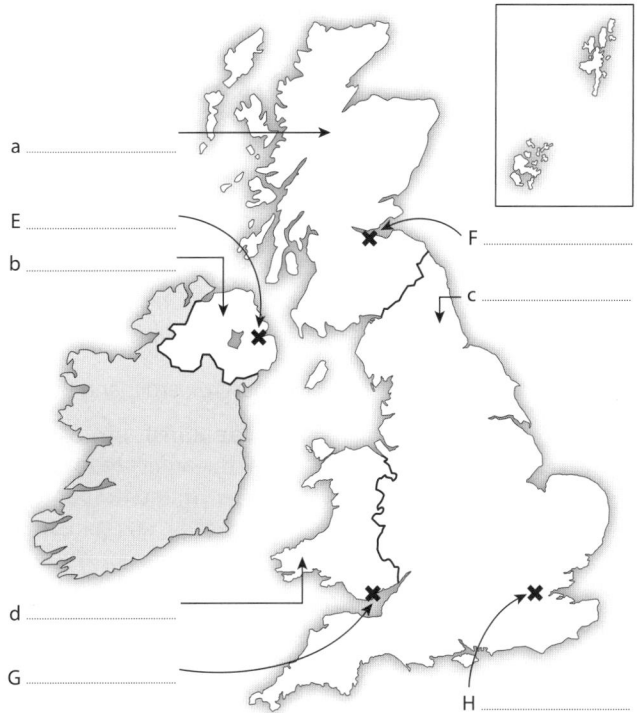

2 Look at the information boxes. Write the names of the countries on them. (1–4)

1 Match the famous places with the pictures.

**Conwy castle   the London Eye
Ben Nevis   the Giant's Causeway**

2 Match each symbol with its country.

a rose   a leek   a shamrock   a thistle

3 Listen to the audio. Write the information you hear in the boxes.

a ....

E ....

b ....

F ....

c ....

d ....

G ....

H ....

1 ....

Population: ....

Famous place: ....

Famous for: ....

....

2 ....

Population: ....

Famous place: ....

Famous for: ....

....

3 ....

Population: ....

Famous place: ....

Famous for: ....

....

4 ....

Population: ....

Famous place: ....

Famous for: ....

....

1.2

What do you know about the UK?

TYPE OF ACTIVITY
Communication as a quiz

LEVEL
Intermediate

TIME
50–60 minutes

AIMS
To enable learners to find out key facts about the UK

VOCABULARY
accent, assembly, divorce rate, dragon, election, gift, patron saint, vote, Gaelic (language), (Government) benefits, Parliament

PREPARATION
One photocopy of the question and the answer card for each pair of learners. Display a large map of the British Isles.

Warmer

Ask learners if they can name the countries of the United Kingdom (England, Scotland, Northern Ireland and Wales). Ask them what the difference is between the British Isles, UK and Great Britain.

> **Answers**
> **The British Isles** is the geographical name for all the islands of England, Scotland, Wales, Northern Ireland and the Republic of Ireland, and includes some other small islands.
> **The United Kingdom** is the name for England, Scotland, Wales and Northern Ireland.
> **Great Britain (or Britain)** is the name for the largest island comprising England, Scotland and Wales.

Identify the four countries of the United Kingdom on the large map. The Republic of Ireland is a separate country. People in the UK generally describe themselves as British and by their country of birth (English, Scottish, Welsh or Irish).

Write two or three familiar statements about the UK on the board. Ask the class which they think they are facts and which are fiction, e.g. *It rains a lot in Britain. British people have a good sense of humour. British people are polite / cold / drink too much.* Tell learners that they are going find out some facts about the UK by doing a quiz from cards containing True/False statements. Pre-teach any new key vocabulary. Divide the class into two groups. Give out Factsheet A to one half of the class, with learners working in pairs or groups of four learners. Give out Factsheet B to the other half. Learners discuss the statements on their cards. They decide together briefly if the information is true or false and mark their responses on the cards. Give out Factsheet A and B answers to the opposite groups.

For the next stage of the lesson, put the pairs of learners together in groups of four (one pair with Factsheet A and another pair with Factsheet B). The pairs take turns to read out each statement, guessing the answers first then exchanging the correct information. The winner is the pair with the most points. Go over the answers with the class and discuss any surprises or interesting points.

Extension

Small groups discuss what they most want to find out about in general, e.g. people's opinions, life in Britain; or what specific topics they would like to cover, e.g. education, food, sport, history, the countryside. You could write a list of topics and ask learners to rate them 1–10. Discuss their suggestions with the class and find out the most popular topics. Explain that you will try to cover their requests in the course.

Factsheet A

Are these statements about the UK true (T) or false (F)?

1   The capital city of Scotland is Cardiff.   **T/F**
2   In the UK, the school leaving age is 15.   **T/F**
3   The patron saint of England is called St George.   **T/F**
4   The second biggest religion in the UK is Islam.   **T/F**
5   In Britain a job centre helps you find work.   **T/F**
6   St Valentine's Day is the Queen or King's official birthday.   **T/F**
7   Queen Elizabeth II married a prince from Greece.   **T/F**
8   Scotland and Northern Ireland have their own languages.   **T/F**
9   The divorce rate in the UK is 45%.   **T/F**
10   The Prime Minister lives in Buckingham Palace.   **T/F**

Factsheet B

Are these statements about the UK true (T) or false (F)?

1   The second biggest city in England is Birmingham.   **T/F**
2   The Welsh language is taught in schools in Wales.   **T/F**
3   40% of Christians in the UK are Catholic.   **T/F**
4   The leader of the government is called an MP.   **T/F**
5   Education is free in the UK.   **T/F**
6   Traditionally, English people eat roast beef and Yorkshire pudding for Saturday lunch.   **T/F**
7   Women have had equal voting rights with men since 1965.   **T/F**
8   Every year it rains and snows more in Rome (Italy) than in London.   **T/F**
9   In 1840, Queen Victoria married a Russian prince.   **T/F**
10   1 in 5 British people are vegetarian.   **T/F**

Factsheet B answers

1   True. Birmingham is England's second biggest city with a population of around a million.
2   True. Welsh is taught in schools and universities and is spoken mostly in North Wales.
3   False. In the UK, about 70% of people say they are Christian but only 10% of them are Catholic.
4   False. The head of government is the PM or Prime Minister. 'MP' means an elected Member of Parliament.
5   True. However, some parents send their children to fee-paying private schools. Some of these are called 'public schools'.
6   False. Traditionally, roast beef and Yorkshire pudding (made with milk, eggs, flour and oil) are eaten together for Sunday lunch.
7   False. Women have had equal voting rights since 1928. Women over 30 got the vote in 1918.
8   True. The annual rain or snow fall in Rome is 750 mm; in London it is 600 mm.
9   False. Queen Victoria married Prince Albert, a German prince.
10   False. Around 1 in 15 people are vegetarian.

Factsheet A answers

1   False. The capital city of Scotland is Edinburgh. Cardiff is the capital of Wales.
2   False. In the UK the school leaving age is 16. Many students go on to further and higher education.
3   True. St George is usually shown killing a dragon. He was probably a Roman soldier from Turkey.
4   True. The 2001 census showed 2.7% Muslims, 1% Hindus, 0.6% Sikhs, 0.5% Jews, 0.3% Buddhists, 20% no religion.
5   True. Jobcentre Plus will help you find work and help you claim some benefits (money to live on while you are unemployed).
6   False. It's a day to send gifts or cards to loved ones and wives and husbands: February 14th.
7   True. The Duke of Edinburgh was born in Greece.
8   True. Scots Gaelic and Irish Gaelic are spoken as a first language by a small minority.
9   True. Nearly 45% of marriages end in divorce.
10   False. The PM lives at 10 Downing Street.

1.3

A view of the UK

TYPE OF ACTIVITY
Listening and information exchange

LEVEL
Advanced

TIME
50–60 minutes

AIMS
To develop an understanding about different aspects of the UK

VOCABULARY
azure, banquet, blunt, clone, consume, delight, draw, gear, missionary, pointer, corporate, high-energy, luscious, quirkiness, stunning, tangible, tedious, the final straw, tranquil

PREPARATION
One copy of the worksheet for each pair of learners cut into sections. Pictures of British cultural life, both positive and negative.

Warmer

Tell learners that they are going to look at some opinions and facts about the UK, reflecting attitudes towards Britain. Learners work in groups of 3–4 and think of their own positive and negative opinions of the UK. Discuss some of the responses with the class.

Show learners pictures of British cultural life. In pairs, learners discuss the positive and negative images that they represent. Tell learners that they are going to hear part of a radio programme in which two people express their opinions about the UK.

▶ 8-9 Dictate questions 1–4 below, then play the audio. Learners take notes and then compare their information with their partners'. Play the audio again, then go over the responses as a class. Discuss the remaining questions 5–7 with the class.

Listening questions

1   Describe the two speakers' attitudes to Britain. What examples do they give?
2   What is the UK's 'unique draw' that the first speaker describes?
3   What are the attractions of British city life to this speaker?
4   What three examples of change does the second speaker give?
5   What do you think about the attitudes expressed by the speakers?
6   How do these comments fit in with your image of the UK?
7   How does this commentary modify your views or your attitudes to the UK?

Answers

1   Speaker 1: positive. The UK has so much to offer, e.g. mountains, beaches, ancient towns and pubs, friendly locals, world class cities.
    Speaker 2: negative. Britain is being systematically destroyed and its individuality is being lost, e.g. quirkiness, history, difference, humour, love of the land, regional variation.
2   The combination of stunning scenery, amazing variety and compact geography.
3   Great music, clubs and food and a thriving art scene.
4   Becoming shaped by 'culture missionaries' whose values are those of big corporations and government; loss of uniqueness and sense of humour; a cloning effect on society.

Option 1: information search

Learners work in groups of four. Pin enlarged images of the information cards around the walls. Give out the information search numbers below (A–D) to each group (on cards). Ask learners to walk round the room to find out what their four numbers represent. They then come together with their group and share their information.

Option 2: group work

Learners work in groups of four. Give each learner an information card and a set of numbers A–D (on cards), face down to each group. Learners read through their information cards and turn over the numbers one by one. The learner with this number tells the group what it refers to.

Information search numbers

A 66, 38, 24, 71	**B** 140,000, 1951, 1.64, 1	**C** 300, 50, 4, 1215	**D** 22, 395, 57, 70

Go over the information with the class. Find out what facts most interested or surprised them. Ask a few questions about the content, e.g. *What percentage of people are worried about debt?* Discuss the implications of this information and invite learners to make comparisons with their own countries.

Extension

Learners could plan to see a film or read a recommended book about the UK. This could continue as a regular 'book/film club night', where a book or film is discussed.

A

140,000 miles of footpaths are found in England & Wales. The public has a right of way on footpaths (on foot) and bridleways (on foot, horseback and cycle).

22 was the age that Charles Darwin formulated the theory of Evolution by Natural Selection during his exploratory world voyage of 1837–9; for 20 years he kept his work secret fearing the outrage it would cause in scientific and religious circles.

1.64 is the 'average number of children' per woman in the UK.

24 UNESCO World Heritage Sites are found in the UK; they include Durham Cathedral, Hadrian's Wall, the Giant's Causeway, St Kilda Island, Caernarfon Castle and parts of Liverpool.

5th position in the world, in terms of GNP (gross national product) is the UK.

66% of people in Britain either own, or are in the process of buying, their own home. Most others live in houses or flats rented from a private landlord or the local council.

57% of homes in the UK have internet access; 81% of adults have mobile phones.

300 languages are spoken in London, making it the most cosmopolitan city in Europe; only New York claims to be as international.

1215 is the date of the Magna Carta, recently described as the greatest constitutional document of all time.

✂ -

B

1% of the UK population owns 70% of the land. 40 million of the 60 million acres of land are owned by the Crown, aristocrats and a few institutions.

395 is the number of people per square km in England, more than 3 times the European average of 117; England is the third most densely populated country in the world after Bangladesh and South Korea.

1951: There are 5 times more people over 85 living now compared to 1951.

4% of births are to teenagers in Britain. It has the highest teenage birth rates in Western Europe – over twice as high as Germany (1.9%) and 4 times as high as Italy (0.9%).

50% of the British population is overweight and 20% obese.

13.1 million British people are in debt; people are increasingly worried about managing their debts and many seek medical help for depression.

70 is the number of times a British citizen is said to be caught on CCTV each day. There is, it is thought, one camera for every 32 people.

38% of British15-year-olds have tried cannabis, compared with 27% in Germany and just 7% in Sweden.

71 is the life expectancy of a male in Glasgow. In one region of the city it drops to 54 years.

2.1

British capital cities

TYPE OF ACTIVITY
Discussion and matching activity

LEVEL
Elementary to Pre-intermediate

TIME
40–50 minutes

AIMS
To find out information about the UK and British symbols

VOCABULARY
botanic garden, castle, cathedral, gallery, library, liquor, museum, palace, quarter, saloon

PREPARATION
Display images of places in the four capital cities. One set of photos for each pair of learners. One set of information cards for each group of four learners.

Warmer

Ask learners to name some famous British cities and check they know the names of the capital cities (Edinburgh, Belfast, Cardiff and London). Ask them one thing they know about each city or the name of any famous places in the cities.

Give out one copy of the photos from the worksheet to each pair. Learners work in pairs to match the building with its name (clues: one building is a castle, one a cathedral, one a grand hall, and the last a modern centre). Learners then match, or guess, the building with the city it is from. Go over the answers with the class.

Option
Display images of these buildings and others, with their names and the cities, on the walls. Learners then walk round the room and match the buildings with the cities.

> **Answers**
> 1 Edinburgh Castle is an ancient castle first built in 1200 on a volcanic rock in Edinburgh, Scotland.
> 2 City Hall is a grand Victorian building, built at the height of the Industrial Revolution. It's now the civic centre in Belfast, Northern Ireland.
> 3 This 'new' St Paul's Cathedral was built after a great fire destroyed old London in 1666.
> 4 The Millennium Building in Cardiff, Wales was opened in 2009 as a centre for art and culture. The inscription above the entrance reads, in English and Welsh: 'In these stones horizons sing'.

Tell learners they are going to read about the four capital cities and ask each other questions about them. Give out one copy of the chart to each learner. In pairs/groups, learners work out the questions they must ask their partners from the prompt words to get the information they require, e.g. *What's the name of your city? What's the population of the city? What's the name of the river? What famous buildings can you see? What can you do there? What festivals are there?* Check the question forms with the class.

Divide the class into groups of four and give each learner in the group information on a different city. Learners read the card and fill in the information about their city. In groups, they ask and answer each other's questions to complete their charts, spelling out words as required. Learners continue the information exchange until they have completed the chart for every city. You could do this as a milling activity: learners walk round the room and exchange information to complete their chart. Go over the answers with the class. Finally, match the buildings from the pictures with the correct Information card. Discuss any points with the class, comparing the cities, e.g. sizes, and any other interesting information.

> **Answers**
> 1 B
> 2 D
> 3 A
> 4 C

Extension

Learners can further develop a British culture blog/book (started in Unit 1a), with the new information about the UK. Learners stick the pictures and information about each UK country onto A4 card.

Match the names of the buildings with the pictures. Do you know which cities they come from?

St Paul's Cathedral	Millennium Centre	City Hall	Edinburgh Castle

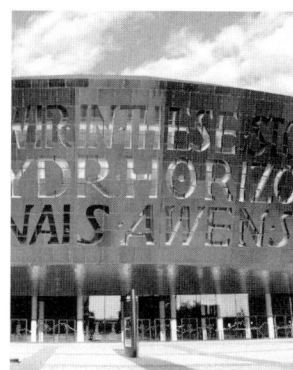

1 ....   2 ....   3 ....   4 ....

✂ -

A London

Population: 7 ½ million

River: the River Thames

Famous buildings: Westminster, St Paul's Cathedral, the 'Gherkin'

Things to do: visit the museums and galleries, go on a river walk or boat trip, go to a West End show

Festivals: Notting Hill Carnival, Lord Mayor's show

B Edinburgh

Population: 488,000

River: the Firth of Forth is near

Famous buildings: Edinburgh Castle, Scottish Parliament, the Old Town

Things to do: go shopping down the Royal Mile, walk to Arthur's Seat and the Royal Botanic Gardens

Festivals: Edinburgh International Festival of Arts

C Cardiff

Population: 328,000

River: the River Taff

Famous buildings: Cardiff Castle, Llandaff Cathedral, the Millennium Centre and stadium

Things to do: visit Cardiff Bay, walk through Bute Park, visit Caerphilly Castle

Festivals: Cardiff Festival, the Mardi Gras festival

D Belfast

Population: 277,000

River: the River Lagan

Famous buildings: City Hall, Grand Opera House, Linen Hall Library

Things to do: visit the Cathedral Quarter and the Titanic Quarter

Festivals: Cathedral Quarter Arts Festival, St Patrick's Day Parade

✂ -

1 City				
2 Population				
3 River				
4 Famous buildings				
5 Things to do				
6 Festivals				

2.2

A profile of London

TYPE OF ACTIVITY
Reading and information gap fill

LEVEL
Intermediate

TIME
50–60 minutes

AIMS
To explore and research London

VOCABULARY
a must, cathedral, century, commerce, cruise, culture, flourish, diversity, huge, invade, medieval, multicultural, plague, playhouse, prosperous, reign, reputation, rise, settlement, site, stop off, trade, tribe, Opera House

PREPARATION
One photocopy of the worksheet for each pair of learners, cut into Card A and Card B. Pictures of London, if available. Flip chart, paper and pens.

Warmer

Write the following words on the board and ask them to guess which city it is: *pie and mash, a double decker bus, the East End, Wembley Stadium, 10 Downing Street, the river Thames, Westminster* (London). Ask learners to work in pairs. They write down other places, objects or facts associated with London. Go over their responses with the class.

Tell learners they are going to find out some interesting facts about London. If you have some pictures of London, show these to the group and elicit any further information that they may know.

Option 1: information exchange (suitable for stronger learners)
Explain that you are going to give pairs of learners two reading cards about London (Cards A and B). Tell them that the information on them is the same but both cards have some information missing. Each learner has to ask their partner questions to find out the missing information. Firstly, ask learners to work in pairs on the same card and work out the questions they will need to ask to find out the missing information. Give an example if necessary, e.g. *The Tower of London was built in …* Question: *When was the Tower of London built?* Learners write their questions down and then form new pairs (Card A with Card B) and ask each other their questions to complete the information gaps. Go through the answers.

Option 2: 'wall dictation' (suitable for less strong learners)
Learners work in groups of four. Give each learner Card A. Learners work out the questions needed to complete the information. Pin A4-size copies of Card B on the walls around the room. (Learners should not be able to read the information from their desks.) One learner from each group goes to the wall chart to find the answer to the question and returns to their group with the answer (in a sentence if possible). Learners complete one space at a time, taking it in turns to go up to the wall chart. They cannot take their card to the wall or remove the information cards from the wall. Go through the answers.

Learners then plan a day out in London in pairs/groups, thinking about famous places they would like to visit and what sites to see, what they would do in the evening, what famous person they would they like to meet for lunch, etc. Give out flip chart paper and pens. Learners feed back their ideas to the class. You could ask learners to go on to plan the ideal day out for the whole class as a discussion activity.

Extension

Learners research some interesting facts about London. To find information, learners can look at Tourist Information sites on the Internet or in guidebooks on Britain. Learners could then prepare a video and record it on a camera. They could then present a TV programme with mini-interviews, news reports and mini-documentaries, explaining about the things they have discovered. Alternatively, learners could continue their research by looking at different cities and towns in Britain. They could then give a brief presentation to the group about the city or town they have researched.

A

A Profile of London

London has a population of [1] .... million. But what kind of city is it to live in? Well, it's a huge city, full of fun and history, and famous for its diversity and culture. London was the world's most visited city in 2006 with over 15 million tourists and it's an exciting mix of creativity, history and fun.

As for its beginnings, originally, an ancient tribe called [2] .... built a settlement here on the river. The Romans made it the capital, after invading in 43 AD, and called it Londinium. By the 3rd century the population was about 30,000.

After the Romans left, in [3] ...., the Vikings, Angles and Saxons moved in, followed by the Norman invasion of 1066. They then began to build hundreds of cathedrals and [4] ...., including the Tower of London.

In 1300, a plague killed at least one third of the inhabitants. It struck again in 1600 and this time over [5] .... people died. Catastrophe hit again in 1666, when the Great Fire of London burnt down most of the old, medieval buildings. So the city was then re-designed and [6] .... was built. By 1700 it was Europe's largest city, with over 600,000 people living, working and trading in it.

London grew very rich in Queen Victoria's reign, from 1837, through trade in tea, [7] .... and then because of the Industrial Revolution. By her death in 1901 the population had risen to 6.6 million.

In the 2nd World War London was [8] .... and afterwards some unattractive buildings were put up. But gradually London became prosperous again, architecture and modern design flourished and it grew into the lively, multicultural centre it is today.

There are so many great places to visit. Just walk along the river Thames from Tower Bridge and visit the Tate Modern gallery, the Globe Theatre, site of [9] ...., stop off at the London Eye and walk over to Westminster Palace. Or, take a cruise to Greenwich and the Observatory, or down to Hampton Court Palace, visiting Kew Gardens on the way.

There's so much more to do too. The British and Kensington Museums, the [10] ...., and Covent Garden, home of the Opera House, are all a must, as well as the West End for shows and shopping!

B

A Profile of London

London has a population of 7 ½ million. But what kind of city is it to live in? Well, it's a huge city, full of fun and history, and famous for its diversity and culture. London was the world's most visited city in 2006 with over [1] .... million tourists and it's an exciting mix of creativity, history and fun.

As for its beginnings, originally, an ancient tribe called the Celts built a settlement here on the river. The Romans made it [2] ...., after invading in 43 AD, and called it Londinium. By the 3rd century the population was about 30,000.

After the Romans left in 410 AD, the Vikings, Angles and Saxons moved in, followed by the [3] .... invasion of 1066. They then began to build hundreds of cathedrals and castles, including the Tower of London.

In 1300, a [4] .... killed at least one third of the inhabitants. It struck again in 1600 and this time over 100,000 people died. Catastrophe hit again in 1666, when the Great Fire of London burnt down most of the old, [5] .... So the city was then re-designed and St Paul's Cathedral was built. By 1700 it was Europe's largest city, with over 600,000 people living, working and trading in it.

London grew very rich in [6] .... reign, from 1837, through trade in tea, coffee and sugar, and then because of the Industrial Revolution. By her death in 1901 the population had risen to [7] ....

In the 2nd World War London was badly bombed and afterwards some unattractive buildings were put up. But gradually London became prosperous again, architecture and modern design flourished and it grew into the lively, [8] .... it is today.

There are so many great places to visit. Just walk along the river Thames from Tower Bridge and visit the Tate Modern gallery, the Globe Theatre, site of Shakespeare's playhouse, stop off at the London Eye and walk over to Westminster Palace. Or, take a cruise to Greenwich and the Observatory, or down to Hampton Court Palace, visiting [9] .... on the way.

There's so much more to do too. The British and Kensington Museums, the markets, and Covent Garden, home of the Opera House, are all a must, as well as the West End for shows and [10] ....!

2.3

TYPE OF ACTIVITY
Reading and listening for information

LEVEL
Advanced

TIME
50–60 minutes

AIMS
To explore the regional and county divisions of the UK

VOCABULARY
blossom, contentious, devolved, disadvantaged, enclosure, establish, identify with, kipper, lambing, marginalised, prosperous, province, remote, reputation, rural, straddle, stretch, World Heritage Site

PREPARATION
Display a map showing the counties and regions of the UK. One photocopy of worksheet for each learner.

Regions and counties of the UK

Warmer

Tell learners that they are going to find out more about the counties and regions of the UK. Give out one copy of the worksheet to each learner. Focus on the map and read through the introductory paragraph. Ask some questions to check comprehension, e.g. *What's the total population of the UK?* (60 million); *What are the main regions of ...?* Describe the population distribution in Wales.

1 ▶ 10–16 Tell learners that they are going to hear some people talking about where they live in Britain. Play the audio for them to write the towns and counties where the seven speakers are from and match the 3 maps with 3 of the speakers. Feed back. Go over the answers with the class.

2 Learners work in pairs. Play the audio again while learners find the answers to the questions. Go over the answers with the class.

Answers

1 1 Newcastle, Northumberland (England)
   2 Chipping Campden, the Cotswolds in the Midlands (England)
   3 Derry/Londonderry (Northern Ireland)
   4 Ullapool in the Highlands of Scotland
   5 St David's, Pembrokeshire coast (south west Wales)
   6 Canterbury, Kent (England)
   7 Liverpool, Merseyside (England)

Maps

   A speaker 5 (Pembrokeshire, Wales)
   B speaker 2 (The Cotswolds, England)
   C speaker 4 (The Highlands, Scotland)

2 1 Speaker 3 (Derry/Londonderry)
   2 Speakers 1 and 2 (shipbuilding on Tyneside; wool in the Cotswolds)
   3 Speaker 6 (Kent – the Garden of England)
   4 Speakers 7 and 2 (Robert Dover's Olympics in the Cotswolds; football teams in Liverpool)
   5 Speaker 5 (St David's)
   6 Speakers 4 and 6
   7 Speaker 5 (dolphins, whales, puffins)
   8 Speaker 1 (Northumberland kings)

3 Learners discuss the questions in small groups or as a class. Tell learners that vowel sounds vary widely from region to region, e.g. southerners say /krɑːft/ while other regions say /kræft/; and Scottish and Northern Irish people often pronounce a final 'r', e.g. *father*. Learners compare northern and southern accents, e.g. Northumberland and Kent, and identify differences in tone, vowel changes, etc. Highlight the use of regional variations in vocabulary: *loch* (lake), *glen* (valley) *aye* (yes), and colloquialisms *like* (Liverpool), cannae (Scotland).

4 Learners look at the final discussion in small groups. There are many regional rivalries across the UK based on a number of social, historical and political reasons and, as in most places, stereotypes exist. For example, people are believed to be more open and friendlier in the north, while southerners are thought to be more reserved.

Extension

Learners can research a province or county in the UK, using the Internet, guide books, etc., and prepare a presentation. Suggested structure: introduction (key facts of population, size, position, administrative centre, most important cities); places of interest (famous cities towns/ buildings and tourist sites); history (historic figures, battles, symbols, importance); geography (climate); and commerce (agriculture and industry).

The countries of the United Kingdom, England, Scotland, Wales and Northern Ireland can be divided into regions, counties and districts.

Geographically, there are several main regions in England: the West Country, a predominantly rural area; the Midlands, once England's major engineering centre; the North, running either side of the Pennine hills; East Anglia, flat agricultural land; and the more prosperous South.

Scotland divides into the southern uplands, the Central Belt which contains over 80% of the population, the sparsely populated Highlands and the remote Western Isles beyond.

In Wales, well over half the population live in mid- and south Wales, and north Wales is mountainous.

Northern Ireland is largely a green agricultural region, similar to the Republic of Ireland in the south.

1 Listen to the audio. Write down the names of the counties and regions on the maps.

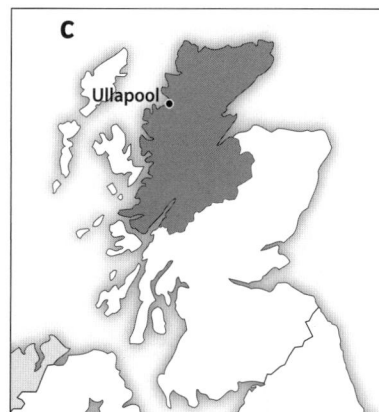

2 Which speaker or speakers mentions the following things? Write down the details.

1 having two names
2 an important industrial history
3 an old nickname
4 a sporting connection
5 being a tiny city
6 beautiful countryside
7 wildlife
8 a royal heritage

3 Discuss the questions with your partner.

1 Which of the seven accents are easy to understand?
2 Which are more difficult? Why do you think this is?
3 What unusual words or expressions can you identify from the audio?

4 In pairs, discuss the questions about accents.

1 Why do you think rivalries exist between different regions in Britain?
2 Do regional rivalries exist in your country? What examples can you give?
3 Tell your partners about the region or district you are from and about your accent or dialect.
4 How important do you think it is to maintain minority languages and dialects in a country?
5 What action would you suggest to prevent the loss of languages and dialects?

HARROW COLLEGE
Learning Centre

3.1

Who lives in the UK?

TYPE OF ACTIVITY
Reading and listening activity

LEVEL
Elementary to Pre-intermediate

TIME
40–50 minutes

AIMS
To develop an understanding of the four British national groups

VOCABULARY
block of flats, east, guitar, north, seaside, south, west, wet, Catholics, Jamaica, Protestants, Rangers (football club), the Caribbean, Yorkshire

PREPARATION
One photocopy of the worksheet for each learner.

Warmer

Ask learners the names of the four countries of the UK (England, Scotland, Wales and Northern Ireland) and the people who live in each country (Scottish, English, Northern Irish, Welsh). Ask them what comes to mind when they think of Scottish, Welsh, English and Irish people. Use sentence scaffolding if required, e.g. *(English) people are … They wear … They work in … They are (appearance) … They live in …* etc.

Give out one worksheet to each learner. Learners work in pairs and focus on exercise A. Learners guess which countries the people in the pictures are from. Ask them why they think this. (Four of the images are stereotypical images: the Scotsman in a kilt, the Welsh person on a sheep farm, the English man in a bowler hat, the Irish woman dancing.) Compare the images with the second pictures and ask them what the differences are. (The other pictures are more realistic.)

Tell learners they are going to find out about four people and where they live. Focus learners on exercise B and go through the instructions. Learners read the first two texts and fill in the missing words, using the word box. Learners check their work in pairs. Go over the answers with the class. As an alternative, learners could read the completed cards to each other.

▶ **17–18** Focus learners on exercise C. They read through the two texts. In pairs, learners guess the missing words. Play the audio for learners to check or complete the gap fill. Go over the answers with the class, checking the pronunciation of any new words. Discuss how people describe their nationality, as appropriate for the group. Refer back to the pictures and ask learners to match the people with the texts.

Answers
A   **1** Scotland   **2** England   **3** Wales   **4** Ireland
B   **1:** Scotland. **1** flats   **2** cold   **3** English   **4** Rangers
     2: Wales. **5** town   **6** mountains   **7** boring   **8** Welsh
C   **3:** Northern Ireland. **1** Northern   **2** names   **3** people   **4** Irish
     4: England. **5** dad   **6** family   **7** work   **8** English

Extension

Ask learners what questions they could ask about a person's everyday life. Write their responses on the board. Prompt with *Where / from? Where / live? How long / live / there? What / job / training? What / house / like?* etc. Tell learners they are going to tell each other about their lives. Learners interview each other, taking notes if appropriate.

Using the Internet or travel books, find some photos of British people in national dress, e.g. a Scotsman wearing a kilt, a Welsh woman in long skirt and hat, an Irish male/female dancer, an English Morris group in country dance clothes (possibly the nearest the English have to a national costume). Learners can produce a page for their British culture blog/book, on British people and their lives.

A Look at the pictures below. Decide which country the people in the pictures are from. Write the country (1–4).

1 .... 2 .... 3 .... 4 ....

B Read about the two British people below.

1 Fill in the gaps in the text.

boring Welsh cold English town mountains flats Rangers

1 ....

I live with my family in a block of
1 .... in Inverness. Scottish
people are quite friendly but the weather is often
2 .... and wet here and
some people don't like that. My dad loves
Scotland and he doesn't like it if you say
he's **3** .... or even British.
My dad just says he's Scottish. I think I'm Scottish
and British… but the most important thing is
I'm a **4** .... fan!

2 ....

My family lives in Harlech, which is a small seaside
5 .... in north Wales.
It's very beautiful here, with the
6 .... behind us but it's
cold and snowy in winter. I work in a local bank,
which is a bit **7** .... but ok.
I play guitar in a band at the weekend and in the
summer I go mountain bike riding. I can speak
8 .... and I say I'm Welsh
too, the same as my family.

C Listen to the audio. Complete the gaps in the texts below.

3 ....

I'm a teacher in a big city in
1 .... Ireland with two
2 .... It's called
Londonderry and Derry. In the past there were
problems between **3** ....
who wanted to be British and people who wanted
to be **4** .... but it's better
now. I just say I'm Northern Irish.

4 ....

I live with my mum and **5** ....
in Birmingham, in England. My mum's from
Yorkshire. She's very funny but has a different
accent to me. We often visit my mum's
6 .... in Leeds. My
grandparents were born in Jamaica, in the Caribbean,
and came here to **7** ....
My dad says he's British but my Mum says she's
8 .... I say I'm black British.

3.2

British men and women

TYPE OF ACTIVITY
Listening, information gap fill and discussion

LEVEL
Intermediate

TIME
40–50 minutes

AIMS
To find out information about British men and women

VOCABULARY
break down, census, class, compulsory, crown, earn, identify, equality, ethnic, evolution, fair, gender, iron, leader, opportunity, produce, right, role, stand up for, suffragette, survival, struggle, the press, vote

PREPARATION
One photocopy of the worksheet for each learner.

Warmer

Tell learners they are going to find out about the lives of men and women in the UK. Write two headings on the board: *British men* and *British women*. Ask learners what they know about the subject and write their responses on the board. Ask if there are any differences between men and women in the UK. Prompt with their wages, education, roles, equal opportunities, lifestyles, attitudes, etc. as required. Ask learners if they were given the right to vote at the same time (no).

1   Give a copy of the worksheet to each learner. Learners work in pairs and guess the answers to the True/False statements. Go over the answers with the class.

> **Answers**
> **a**   F: Men earn more in general but tax paid on income is the same for everyone.
> **b**   F: Margaret Thatcher was the first female British PM from 1979–90.
> **c**   T: The law requires equal pay for the same job.
> **d**   T: 31.6 million women out of a total population of 62.7 million.
> **e**   F: Women have fewer accidents and used to pay lower car insurance than men.
> **f**   T: However, this is gradually being changed over the next decade.

2   **Option 1: jigsaw listening (suitable for stronger learners)**

> ▶ 19   Learners fold the time ladder in half. One half of the class reads through Part 1 of the time ladder (a–i). The other half of the class reads Part 2 (1–9). Ask learners to start from the bottom of the ladder. As they read learners guess some of the missing words. Play the audio for learners do the gap fill activity on their half only. Give out the answers to each part of the class for learners to check their answers together. Learners make new Part 1/Part 2 pairs and exchange their information. They can do this by asking questions, e.g. *What happened in ...? What age did ....?* or listening to the text read by their partner. Learners fill in the gaps. Play the audio once more to check answers. Discuss the differences found between men's and women's lives in the UK and any surprises.

Option 2: pairwork gap fill (suitable for less strong learners)

> ▶ 19   Tell learners they are going to listen to a talk comparing British men and women's lives and history. Pre-teach key vocabulary. Learners read through the time ladder together and guess the missing words. Alternatively, you could write the missing vocabulary on the board and ask learners to fill in the gaps. Play the audio for learners to complete the gap fill or check their answers. Discuss the differences found between men's and women's lives in the UK.

> **Answers**
> **a** 10   **b** seat   **c** fought   **d** women   **e** equal   **f** Iron Lady   **g** MP   **h** jobs   **i** less
> **1** 24%   **2** MP   **3** school   **4** average   **5** jobs   **6** marriages   **7** problems   **8** 1990
> **9** a third

3   Learners discuss the questions on the worksheet in small groups. Go over their responses with the class, drawing out inequalities for men as well as women. Discuss any further points of interest.

Extension

Use the questionnaire from the worksheet to develop some key topics further, e.g. women at war, women and ethnicity, men and voting rights. Learners look at social history websites and produce a short report to add to their British culture book/blog. They could also produce a time line of social development for their own countries, finding out data on men and women's earnings, career choices, etc. Activities around migration to the UK can be found in *ESOL Activities Entry 3*.

1 In pairs decide if these statements are true (T) or false (F).

  1 Men pay more tax than women in the UK.   T/F

  2 There has never been a female Prime Minister.   T/F

  3 Pay for men and women is the same.   T/F

  4 Women outnumber men in the UK.   T/F

  5 British men are safer drivers than women.   T/F

  6 Women retire earlier than men.   T/F

2 You are going to hear a talk about men and women in Britain.

  1 Read through the 'time ladder' statements from the bottom step to the top (a–i and 1–9) Guess the missing words.

  2 Listen and see if you were correct.

Part 1: British women

i Research shows that women still earn .... than men.

h PM Tony Blair gave more .... to women in the Labour government of 1997.

g Diane Abbott became the first British black woman .... in 1987.

f Margaret Thatcher became the first female Prime Minister in 1979 and was known as the ....

e Women wrote about equality and demanded .... rights at work and equal pay in the 60s.

d The new Waterloo Bridge in London was built mostly by .... in 1942.

c Emmeline Pankhurst .... for the right of women to vote. Women got the vote in 1918.

b The first woman to take a .... as an MP was Lady Astor, a conservative, in 1919.

a In 1837 Queen Victoria was crowned. Education became compulsory for boys and girls up to the age of ....

Part 2: British men

9 Only .... of men in Britain do housework even if both partners are working full time.

8 In .... Justin Fashanu became the first openly gay male footballer.

7 In the 1990s men's groups became a way for men to discuss .... such as their role as fathers.

6 Men fought for more legal rights to see their children if their .... ended.

5 Most major government .... went to men. Eton public school has produced 20 Prime Ministers.

4 In World War II, the .... age of a pilot was only 20.

3 In 1918 .... was made compulsory for boys and girls up to the age of 14.

2 Dadabhai Naoroji became the first Asian male .... in Britain in 1892.

1 In 1880 any man with land valued at £10 could vote but this only added up to .... of the population.

3 Discuss the following questions with a partner.

  1 What do you think of the position of women and gender equality in the UK?

  2 How is it similar to the situation in your country? How is it different?

  3 In general, how equal are people in most societies?

  4 How important do you think it is for men and women to be treated equally? Why?

3.3

Minority groups in Britain

TYPE OF ACTIVITY
Listening, reading and discussion

LEVEL
Advanced

TIME
50–60 minutes

AIMS
To find out about different groups of people in the UK

VOCABULARY
background, characteristic, culture, multicultural, personal identity, personal qualities, stereotype, British Asian, Afro-Caribbean

PREPARATION
One photocopy of the worksheet for each learner.
Display pictures of different ethnic and cultural groups from the UK.

Warmer

Write the word *culture* on the board. Learners discuss and write a definition in pairs/groups. They then discuss what *culture* can refer to (in the context of their English course) and put their ideas on a spidergram, with arrows pointing to possible areas, e.g. *art, language, tradition, food, religion, history, religion, dance, music*. Briefly discuss the charts and explore other categories that may have been suggested, e.g. *beliefs, values, laws, attitude, meaning, a sense of place, identity, rituals, habits*.

1   Give a copy of the worksheet to each learner. Focus on the definitions of *culture* and ask which they prefer. Learners look at the pictures and describe to their partner what they represent (Notting Hill carnival and a Hindu wedding). Go over their responses. Read the introductory text and ask one or two information questions, e.g. *What is the general British attitude to minority groups? How is multiculturalism reflected in the UK?* Explain that a census has taken place every ten years in the UK since 1801. The last one was in 2011.

2   ▶ 20–22 Focus learners on the table. They take notes under the headings as they listen, then compare their answers. Feed back.

Answers

	The Clarkes	The Sharmas	Reza and Ellie
Names, place of birth, age	Beverley: 50s; Camberwell, London Delroy: 50s; Jamaica	Sushil: 80; India Raj: 45; India Elisha: 10; Scotland	Reza: 30; Iran Ellie: 37; Poland
Work history	Beverley: teacher trainer Delroy: self-employed builder Son: works for BT Daughter: interpreter	Sushil: retired teacher, came to UK when wife died Raj: IT specialist, single parent, carer Elisha: schoolgirl, thinks of herself as Scottish and Indian	Reza: refugee who became business graduate working for local company Ellie: came as migrant worker, now assistant manager in care home
Religion / beliefs	Both are keen churchgoers	Hindu Raj is vegetarian	Reza: Muslim Ellie: Catholic Neither is strict about religion
National identity, ethnicity	Beverley: Londoner Delroy: Black British Children: Black British Caribbean	Sushil: British Raj: British Asian Elisha: Scottish and Indian	Reza: British passport but thinks of himself as Azari (region of Iran) Ellie: Polish

3   Learners go through the discussion questions in pairs or groups and feed back to the class.

Extension

Learners research information on cultural identity in Britain and can make comparisons between their country and Britain on the topics identified in the warmer activity. As a follow up, they can choose a context or topic to present to the class.

Some very interesting films to watch on ethnic identity, values and class include *West is West, Secrets and Lies, My Beautiful Launderette, Brick Lane, This is England*.

culture *n.* the way of life, especially the general customs and beliefs, of a particular group of people at a particular time
culture *n.* music, art, theatre, literature, etc.
cultural *adj.* relating to the habits, traditions and beliefs of a society

1 Read the text about British culture.

Walk around any British town centre and the history of immigration to Britain is obvious. Its legacy and impact is reflected in the myriad of international restaurants, shops and market stalls that can be found in even small towns. Britain has a long history of immigration and it's not unusual to see Polish food in corner shops alongside pasta and curry powder.

Minority groups represent about 10% of the population over the whole of the UK. On a day-to-day basis British people are generally relatively tolerant to migrants and it's more likely

political and social events that raise their profile. In the press, one person described it as 'a kind of occasional intolerance mixed with indifference'.

2011 Census

On 27th March 2011, the whole nation was asked to fill in a form describing their lives, their education and work status and their national identity. Questions included: *How would you describe your national identity? What's your ethnic group? What's your job? What's your religion?*

2 You are going to hear some people talking about their backgrounds and identity. Listen and complete the table about each family/person.

	The Clarkes	The Sharmas	Reza and Ellie
Names, place of birth, age			
Work history			
Religion / beliefs			
National identity, ethnicity			

3 Discuss the questions with a partner.

- What do you find particularly interesting about each story?
- What's the difference between a person's identity and their national identity?
- How would you describe your identity? What about your national identity?
- What do you consider the characteristics of people from your country?
- What minority groups do you have in your country? What issues does this raise in your society?
- What is the problem of discussing cultural groups in terms of generalisations?
- What is your view of the concept of multicultural societies?

A guide to the British Government

Warmer

Ask learners if they know the name of the British Prime Minister and the names of any political parties or politicians in the UK. Write their responses on the board (the main parties are Conservatives, Labour and the Liberal Democrats). Ask learners if they know if Britain has a president. (No; the Queen or King is the constitutional head of state but has no power.) Tell learners they are going to find out more about important places and people in the British government. This activity can be delivered in two different ways.

Option 1: wall dictation (suitable for stronger learners)
Pin the four information cards around the room (as A4 size posters). Learners work in pairs. Give out one copy of the question card to each pair of learners for them to read through. Learners then go up to the posters, find the answers to the questions and write these down. Go over the answers with the class and discuss any other points arising.

Option 2: table group work (suitable for less strong learners)
Learners work in groups of 3–4. Give out one set of cards per group. They match the text with the pictures and addresses. Check the answers with the class. Then give out the question cards. Learners find the answers. Go over their answers with the class and discuss any points arising.

TYPE OF ACTIVITY
Matching activity and information search

LEVEL
Elementary to Pre-intermediate

TIME
40–50 minutes

AIMS
To develop an awareness of British political institutions

VOCABULARY
assembly, elect, election, government, head, law, leader, make a change, mayor, monarch, palace, parliament, prime minister, politician, power, speech, terraced, vote

PREPARATION
Display pictures of some British government buildings, if available. One copy of the question card for each learner. Option 1: cut up and enlarge the four information cards. Option 2: photocopy one set of information cards for each table of 3–4 learners. Cut addresses from each reading card to make a set.

Answers
1 10 Downing Street
2 7.5 million
3 City Hall, The Queen's Walk, London
4 Westminster Palace by the River Thames
5 the Queen or King
6 five years
7 power
8 make London a better place
9 yes
10 Sir Robert Walpole
11 assemblies
12 opens Parliament

This is an opportunity to work on the pronunciation and stress of words of two or three syllables. Write the words up across the board. Learners work in pairs and write the words in two different columns: those with two syllables (one strong and one weak stress) in the left column and three syllables (one strong and two weak stresses) in the right column. (See the completed chart below. The sound in a strong stress is higher-pitched and longer.)

Word stress	Xx	Xxx
	Country	parliament
	Labour	Westminster
	Building	government
	Council	Buckingham
	Palace	minister

Extension

Learners continue working on the British culture book/blog. They could also include pictures and short texts about the Scottish Government and the Assembly buildings in Wales and Northern Ireland. A good site at this level is www.parliament.uk/education/online-resources.

If learners are in Britain, plan a trip to London and visit Downing Street, take a tour inside Parliament, see the London Council buildings and visit Buckingham Palace. If this is not possible, take a virtual tour of 10 Downing Street on www.10-downingstreet.gov.uk and of the Queen's opening of Parliament at www.royalcollection.org.uk.

1 Find the correct answers to the questions and complete the sentences.

1 Where does the Prime Minister live? ....

2 What's the population of London? ....

3 Where does the Mayor of London work? ....

4 Where are the Houses of Parliament? ....

5 Who is the head of state of the United Kingdom? ....

6 In the UK, there is an election every ....

7 The monarch has no .... but is very important.

8 What does the Mayor of London help to do? ....

9 Can a woman become the Mayor of London? ....

10 The first PM of Britain was ....

11 Wales and Northern Ireland both have ....

12 What does the King or Queen do after the summer holiday?

---

10 Downing Street,
London
SW1A 2AA

The Prime Minister lives in a flat at number 10 Downing Street, in Westminster, London. Britain's first Prime Minister, Sir Robert Walpole, lived here too in 1730.

There is an election in the UK every five years. If there is a new Prime Minister, he or she moves into this famous terraced house that is very near to Parliament. The PM's offices are also here.

You can look around No. 10 if you go online to www.10-downingstreet.gov.uk.

The Houses of Parliament,
Westminster Palace,
London

Many important government offices are in a part of London called Westminster. The two Houses of Parliament are in Westminster Palace, by the river Thames.

In the House of Commons the government makes new laws for the country. Then the House of Lords looks at these laws again and talks about them for a second time.

Scotland also has a parliament. Wales and Northern Ireland have assemblies. They have less power but are important in these countries.

City Hall
The Queen's Walk
London
SE1 2AA

The Mayor of London has a very important job. He or she is a politician who works in City Hall on the river Thames and helps to make London a nice, safe place for people to live and work in.

The people of London vote for a new mayor every five years. The population of London is now over 7 ½ million and the Mayor and the London Assembly can make a lot of changes in London to try to make people's lives better.

Buckingham Palace Rd
Westminster
London
SW1A 1AA

The head of state of the United Kingdom is the Queen or King. After an election, the new Prime Minister goes to the Palace and asks the monarch if he or she can make a new government.

Every year, after the summer holiday, the Queen or King opens Parliament and reads a speech about the new laws that the government wants to make. The monarch has no power but is very important and meets the leaders of many other countries.

4.2

TYPE OF ACTIVITY
Reading and information search

LEVEL
Intermediate

TIME
50–60 minutes

AIMS
To find out about the British political system

VOCABULARY
assembly, candidate, citizen, civil servant, coalition, debate, democracy, democratic, first-past-the-post, elect, hung parliament, inherit, life peer, lord, mayor, minority government minister, Prime Minister, party, proposal, seat, vote, the Cabinet, the Houses of Parliament, the Speaker, Westminster

PREPARATION
Display pictures of the interior of the two Houses of Parliament, the Prime Minister, the Cabinet, etc. Enlarge the worksheet to A3 size, if possible and photocopy one worksheet for each group of learners, cut into sets of questions and texts.

Everyday politics

Warmer

Tell learners they are going to look at the political system in the UK. Write the title, *Politics in the UK* on the board as a spidergram. Ask learners what vocabulary or expressions they know associated with politics, particularly, British politics.

Working in pairs or threes, learners write down one or two questions they would like to ask about the British system, e.g. *How often do people vote? Who can become an MP?* Learners could stick their questions onto flip chart paper pinned on the wall to be checked at the end of the lesson. The activity can be delivered in two different ways.

Option 1: question card game (suitable for stronger learners)
Learners work in groups of three or four. The question cards are spread face down on the table and the reading cards are placed face up on the table or pinned to a wall. Learners take turns to pick up a question and read it to the group. The groups race to find the answer. The learner holding the question writes their response down. Go over the answers as a class and discuss any further questions.

Option 2: question and answer pair activity (suitable for less strong learners)
Learners work in pairs or threes. Give out a set of reading cards with the questions cut up in twos (questions 1 and 2 together, 3 and 4 together, etc). Learners match the pairs of questions with the information cards, then scan the cards to find the answers and write them down. Go over the answers as a class and discuss any further questions.

> **Answers**
> 1 Conservatives, Liberal Democrats and Labour Party
> 2 they hold party conferences
> 3 18 or over
> 4 the candidate who gets the most votes and the party with the most seats
> 5 about 20
> 6 they make important decisions or proposals to discuss in Parliament
> 7 650
> 8 look at new laws and suggest changes
> 9 to give citizens in other parts of the UK more control over their own affairs
> 10 legislate for country-specific matters such as education
> 11 in town halls and county halls
> 12 many local public services from environmental health to parks, libraries and sports centres

Learners compare the British system with the political systems of their own countries and feed back to the class or group.

Extension

Learners research aspects of the British political system using the websites below. Suggested topics include: the House of Lords, the PM, the Chancellor of the Exchequer, the Cabinet, the Civil Service, local government, the European Union, etc. Learners make a short report, a video programme or presentation on these topics.

For more information on parliament and government in the UK, see www.10-downingstreet.gov.uk; www.parliament.uk; www.directgov.org. *ESOL Activities Entry 3* also has a range of further activities as well as information on British Culture and Citizenship.

1 What are the three main parties in the UK?

2 What do the parties do every year?

3 At what age can you vote in the UK?

4 Who wins an election in Parliament?

5 How many ministers sit in the Cabinet?

6 What does the Cabinet do?

7 How many MPs are there in the Commons?

8 What do members of the House of Lords do?

9 Why were devolved parliament and assemblies set up?

10 What do the devolved authorities do?

11 Where do local councils meet?

12 What do local councils organise?

British political parties

In Britain anyone can become an MP but usually people belong to a political party. The three main parties in the UK are the Conservatives, the Liberal Democrats and the Labour party. There are also parties in Scotland, Northern Ireland and Wales that are represented in the British Parliament. Every year the parties hold party conferences to debate their views and future plans. You can write to, or visit, your MP if you have a real problem and need their support.

The electoral system in the UK

Every five years there is a general election to form a government. If you are 18 or over, you are allowed to vote. MPs represent constituencies and are chosen by a first-past-the-post system. The candidate who gets the most votes wins a seat in Parliament and the party with the most seats wins the election. If no party wins a majority, it's called a 'hung' parliament but a minority government or coalition can govern. When people disagree with the government they can protest by signing petitions and attending marches and rallies.

How the British Government works

Politicians work at the Houses of Parliament, at Westminster in London. The Prime Minister appoints a Cabinet (a team) of about 20 senior MPs or ministers, including the Chancellor of the Exchequer, Home Secretary, Foreign Secretary and Minister for Education. The Cabinet meets weekly and makes important decisions or proposals for new laws which are then debated in Parliament. Civil servants continue the work of the government from office buildings in an area called Whitehall.

The Houses of Parliament

The government is based in two 'Houses' at the Palace of Westminster, known as the Houses of Parliament. In the House of Commons, which is controlled by the Speaker, there are 650 elected Members of Parliament who make new laws. The House of Lords advises on the work of the House of Commons. All new laws are proposed by the Commons and then approved by the Lords, who may request changes. There are around 850 peers. Some have inherited titles, others are experts who become Lords, known as 'life peers' because their title ends when they die.

The government systems in Scotland, Wales and Northern Ireland

In order to give citizens in other parts of the UK more local control, a parliament in Scotland and two new assemblies in Wales and Northern Ireland were set up in the 1990s. Their politicians discuss local affairs and they have different powers. For example, they make decisions on their legal and education systems.

Local government in Britain

In the UK, local councillors are elected every four years. Councillors mostly belong to political parties but some are elected independently. Local councils meet in Town Halls and County Halls all over the country and make local rules and regulations for their area. They organise many local public services from environmental health to parks, libraries and sports centres, which people pay for in a Council Tax. The head of the local council in England is the Mayor.

4.3

TYPE OF ACTIVITY
Reading, listening and discussion

LEVEL
Advanced

TIME
50–60 minutes

AIMS
To find out about parliament and government in the UK

VOCABULARY
commoner, life peer, noble, the House of Commons, the House of Lords, the Speaker

PREPARATION
Take in advanced level dictionaries. One copy of the worksheet for each pair of learners. Flip charts and pens. Option: copies of the script

How the government works

Warmer

Tell learners they are going to look at the British political system. Ask if they can name any political parties or key figures in British politics, e.g. the Conservative party, the Labour party, the Liberal Democrats, the Green party; the Prime Minister, the Leader of the Opposition, the (Shadow) Home Secretary, the Speaker. If learners are more familiar with the British system, working in small groups, they write down (or draw) what they know about the structure of British government and the parliamentary system. Go over these with the class.

1   Give out one copy of the worksheet to each learner. Focus learners on the image of Westminster. Tell them there are over 700 members of the House of Lords and that the Commons has 650 MPs (Members of Parliament) but can only seat about 400 of them – that's why MPs stand for important debates and votes. Then focus learners on the reading. Working in pairs, learners read the article and answer the questions. Learners look at the words in italics and discuss their meanings. Check the vocabulary with the class. Go over answers with the class.

> **Answers**
> **1   1** *parler*: talk (from French, the language of the educated classes at the time); *commoners*: ordinary people; *nobles*: titled people; *curtailed*: put a stop to/ended; *life peers*: lords for their lifetime; *political bias*: leaning towards one political party or group; *scrutiny*: close inspection
> **2** Commons: to create new bills (laws); Lords: debate and examine new bills
> **3** from two of the King's councils of commoners and nobles in medieval times
> **4** advantage: a two-house system is a good check on abuse of power; disadvantage: in Britain one house (Lords) is unelected by the general public (and therefore undemocratic)

2   ▶ 23 Focus learners on exercise 2, the audio on Prime Minister's questions. Explain that every week the PM has to answer questions from the opposition and other MPs and that traditionally there is a noisy and confrontational atmosphere. Other debates in the House are usually not like this although it can be noisy and adversarial. Learners read through questions 1–4. You may wish to pre-teach some vocabulary from the audio: *devolving, manifesto, constituency, philanthropic giving, thriving communities, volunteering*.

Play the audio while learners write their responses. Learners check their answers in pairs. Go over these with the class. Play the audio again for learners to think about the atmosphere in the house, and the exchanges taking place, in pairs or as a class. Option: give out copies of the script for learners to study.

> **Answers**
> **2   1** £200 million   **2** Sure Start is a government initiative supported by parent volunteers; 250 are expected to close   **3** the Big Society is a government initiative to open up public services to more local involvement and control   **4** that these changes will have a negative affect on communities

3   Learners discuss the questions about the debate itself. Go over their responses with the class. In exercise 4, learners work in small groups, discussing the question and quotations. Go over their responses with the class and discuss any points arising.

Extension

Learners hold a debate in the style of PMQs on a relevant issue, taking on roles of the Prime Minister, the Speaker, Leader of the Opposition and backbenchers. Research key topics in British government. Useful sites are: www.parliament.uk; www.10-downingstreet.gov.uk; www.10downingstreet.gov.uk; BBC and newspaper websites.

1 Read the text on the British parliamentary system and answer the questions below.

1 Discuss the meanings of the words in *italics*.

Today's British Parliament developed from the historic councils of its medieval kings. In order to '*parle*' with the king, knights and town's representatives, or *commoners*, would gather in one space in the Palace and *nobles* and church leaders in another. Thus the two Houses of Parliament, the House of Commons and the House of Lords, were created.

They have since existed side by side in the Palace of Westminster for hundreds of years. However, in the 20th century the House of Commons successfully *curtailed* the power of the unelected House of Lords.

The creation of *life peers* from politicians, educationalists, scientists, philanthropists and people in sport and the arts, adjusted the historic *political bias* of the Lords to make it a more representative institution.

Today the House of Lords is a place of debate and discussion, with limited powers of delay, where bills are examined and returned to the House of Commons for further *scrutiny* by the government.

2 What are the roles of the two Houses?

3 How did the two-house system first develop?

4 What are the advantages and disadvantages of this system?

2 Listen to the excerpt from Prime Minister's question time. Answer the questions below.

1 How much money does he say will be put into the 'Big Society bank'?

2 How is Sure Start supported by the community? How many are expected to close?

3 What is the Big Society?

4 What is the Opposition's concern?

3 In groups, describe and discuss the following aspects of the audio.

- the atmosphere in the House of Commons
- the relationship between the parliamentarians and the PM and the role of the Speaker
- the content and quality of the exchanges between politicians

4 Discuss the following questions in your groups.

- Compare these exchanges with what happens in your country.
- What do you think of the adversarial approach of British politics?
- How important is debate in such political institutions?
- What would you suggest to be a better way of making laws in a country?

5 Read the quotes below. What are they suggesting? Do you agree?

I do not object to people looking at their watches when I am speaking. But I strongly object when they start shaking them to make certain they are still going. *Lord Birkett (1960)*

If politics is theatre, then this is the cast ... *(The Parliamentary website)*

Reporter: Minister, are you going to run for the leadership of your party?

Minister: How many times do I have to tell you? No! No! No!

Reporter: So you haven't entirely ruled it out. (Journalist's joke)

5.1

The Royal Family

TYPE OF ACTIVITY
Listening and information search

LEVEL
Elementary to Pre-intermediate

TIME
40–50 minutes

AIMS
To find out about the history and role of the royal family

VOCABULARY
government, head of state, law, marry, member, minister, monarch, nearby, palace, power, royal, title, Welsh, Scots

PREPARATION
One copy of the worksheet for each learner. Display images of UK kings and queens from the past to the present.

Warmer

Ask learners if they can tell you the opposite word for a *king* (*queen*) and a *prince* (*princess*). Ask if the UK has a king or a queen and if they know their name(s). Elicit information about them or display an image of the royal family. Tell learners that the UK is a *monarchy* (i.e. a king or queen is the head of state). Ask if they can name any previous queens or kings. Prompt with images as required, e.g. Queen Victoria, Henry VIII, Elizabeth I.

1   Give out a copy of the worksheet to each learner. Focus learners on the first activity. Learners work in pairs and match the words or titles for men and women. Go over answers with the class. Explain the status of each title, as required.

You could display images of current members of the Royal Family doing different activities (e.g. Royal weddings, state opening of Parliament). Ask who they are and what they're doing.

> **Answers**
> **1**
> **King/Queen**: The king's wife is called 'queen' but the reigning queen's husband isn't called 'king'.
> **Prince/Princess**: the sons and daughters of the king or queen; the brothers and sisters of the monarch; the husband of the reigning queen.
> **Duke/Duchess**: the highest title after the monarch; also used by members of the royal family.
> **Lord/Lady**: a title sometimes given to ordinary people from the community, members of the aristocracy, important church people, non-elected and elected members of the House of Lords.
> **Sir/Madam**: formal, polite ways to address men and women; *Sir* is a title sometimes given to men for good things done for society; the female equivalent is *Dame*.
> **Mr/Mrs**: common formal titles for a man and a married woman (*Ms* is used for an adult woman and doesn't show her marital status; *Miss* is used for an unmarried woman or young girl).

2   ▶ 24   Tell learners they are going to read an article about the British royal family. Focus learners on exercise 2. Tell them there are some gaps in the text. Working in pairs, learners read the article and try to fill in or guess the gaps. Play the audio for learners to check and go over the answers with the class. Play a second time if required.

3   Focus learners on exercise 3, questions 1–5. Ask them to find the answers to the questions in the text. Go over the answers together.

> **Answers**
> **2**
> **1** lives   **2** castle   **3** Head   **4** opens   **5** make   **6** work   **7** lives
> **8** England   **9** Wales   **10** crowned   **11** Prince   **12** 200
> **3**
> **1** Egbert   **2** open Parliament, meet with presidents, make speeches, visit different countries   **3** no, Parliament does   **4** at Buckingham Palace   **5** Windsor

4   Focus learners on the discussion. Ask learners what they know about their countries'/other royal families, e.g. their history, what they do, where they live, how old they are. Discuss any further questions about the kings and queens of England/the UK, both past and present.

Extension

Learners make a family tree with photos of the British royal family and information about each person to add to their British culture blog/book. Refer to the website www.royal.gov.uk for key facts, e.g. Who was the first queen? Why does the UK still have a royal family? Look at the list of monarchs on the website: www.kingsandqueens.gov.uk. Watch Queen Elizabeth's coronation and other royal occasions on the Internet.

1 Write the correct pairs of words together.

Man   Woman

....

....

....

....

....

Sir · Duchess · Mrs · King · Princess · Lady · Lord · Madam · Duke · Mr · Prince · Queen

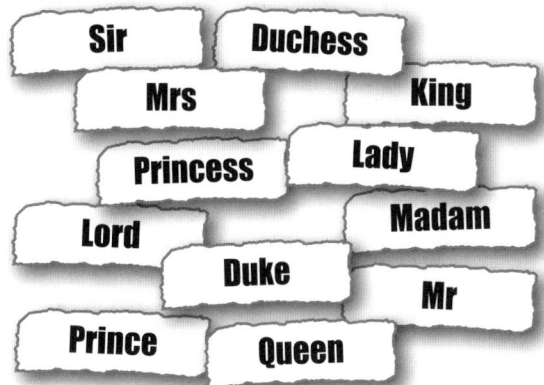

2 Read the text about the British royal family.

1 Fill in the gaps.

2 Listen to the audio for the answers.

The British royal family's surname is Windsor. The queen ¹ .... at Buckingham Palace in London and other family members live nearby. They go to Balmoral, a ² .... in Scotland, every year on holiday.

The king or queen is the ³ .... of State. They have no real power but are still important. He or she ⁴ .... Parliament, meets with presidents and heads of state, and visits different countries. The Prime Minister and the government ⁵ .... new laws. Every week the Prime Minister goes to see the king or queen at Buckingham Palace to talk about the ⁶ .... that the government is doing.

In the past, kings and queens had a lot of power and had very different ⁷ .... Some fought and died in battle at home and abroad. Others, like King Charles I, were executed.

King Egbert was the first 'King of all ⁸ .... in the 9th century. A tough English king called Edward I took control of ⁹ .... , in 1282. The crowns of Scotland and England joined together in 1603, after Elizabeth I died. She had no children so James VI of Scotland, the son of Mary, Queen of Scots, was ¹⁰ .... James I of England, Scotland, Ireland and Wales. The oldest son of the king or queen is called the ¹¹ .... of Wales but there is no Welsh King now. There have been over ¹² .... kings and queens altogether.

3 Find the answers to the questions in the text.

1 Who was the first king of England?

2 What four important things must the monarch do?

3 Does the king or queen make the laws in the UK?

4 Where do the Royal Family live?

5 What's the family name of the British royal family?

4 Discuss the questions in your groups.

• What other things do you know about the British royal family?

• Do you have a royal family in your country?

• What other things do kings and queens do?

• Is it a good or bad idea to have royal families? Why do you think this?

5.2

British families

TYPE OF ACTIVITY
Reading, listening, gap fill and discussion

LEVEL
Intermediate

TIME
50–60 minutes

AIMS
To explore the range of British family structures

VOCABULARY
assist, baby-sitter, birth, civil ceremony, home help, hourly rate, foster carer, get/be married/ divorced, increase, marry (someone), mixed-race, occasional, pattern, reference, statistic, step-parent, town hall

PREPARATION
One photocopy of the worksheet for each learner.

Warmer

Ask learners if anyone has ever stayed with a family in the UK. Find out what they know about typical British families, e.g. *What's the average number of children couples have in the UK?* (2) *What social things do families do? Do many people get divorced in the UK?* Alternatively, focus learners on two contrasting pictures of British families, as available, and ask learners to imagine some information about them, e.g. *How many children have they got? What's the father's/mother's job? How much do they earn? Where do they live? Where were the parents or children born? Does the mother work? Where does the family go on holiday? Where do the children's grandparents live?*

1   Tell learners they are going to find out about some different family groups in the UK. Give out one copy of the worksheet to each learner. Focus on exercise 1. Learners work in pairs, matching the images and the texts. Go over the answers with the class. Ask some concept questions to check their understanding, e.g. *What kind of texts are they? Who wrote them?* Look at the range of family structures in the UK. Discuss any surprises, questions and opinions with the class.

> **Answers**
> **1**
> 1d   2c   3a   4b
> **Contexts**
> **1** child: school work or letter   **2** grandmother: writing to her grandchild   **3** single father: a job advert in a newspaper   **4** a co-habiting couple: an invitation to a wedding

2   Learners read through the text and fill in the gaps, using the word box. Go over the answers with the class.

> **Answers**
> **1** both   **2** 45   **3** single   **4** 10   **5** later   **6** elderly

3   Develop a discussion about this information using the following prompts, e.g. *Why do you think the UK has a high divorce rate? What do you think about step-parents / foster parents? Why do you think so many people live alone in the UK?* Learners then do the discussion activity in small groups. Feed back their opinions to the class for general discussion.

Extension

Watch a clip of a film or video showing British family life. You could use a British soap such as *Eastenders* or comedy such as *Outnumbered*. Pre-set questions about daily life, the role of the parents, the behaviour of the children and general politeness. Discuss learners' opinions and any comparisons made.

Learners can also prepare a page for their British culture book/blog on British family life. They could include examples of different types of family structures, information on elderly people and children, with facts and figures given in the form of charts or graphs. The 2011 Census (online) shows data about families. *ESOL Activities Entry 1, 2 and 3* also have interesting facts and activities on family life.

1 Match the texts with the pictures.

a

b

c

d

1 ....

> I live with my two mums, Sue and Kate. My granny and grandpa live about 20 minutes away. My mum had a civil partnership ceremony last year, like a wedding, in the Town Hall. I have a dad too who's around a lot.

2 ....

> Dear Jordan,
> I'm much better after my fall last week. The carers have been very nice here. I hope to see you all next weekend and we can go for a nice drive in the country.
> All my love
> Granny

3 ....

> ### Wanted
> Home help wanted to assist with cooking, cleaning and collecting 12 yr old daughter from school. 41 yr old male single parent works locally. Hrs 3-6pm Mon-Fri. Good hourly rate for right lady
> **References and experience required**

4 ....

> *Wedding Invitation*
> Getting married after 10 years!
> We'd love you to join us and the kids to celebrate our wedding …
> Sam & Kelly

2 Read the text on family life in the UK and complete the gaps with the words below.

single   later   both   45   elderly   10

Report on family life in the UK

Families are traditionally 'nuclear' in the UK. This means they consist of a father, a mother and the children but over the last 40 years British families have changed dramatically. This is because of the rise in divorce and the changing attitudes to different types of family units. Recent statistics show that:

- 65% of children live with [1] .... their parents
- [2] ....% of couples get divorced – this figure drops to 30% after 20 years of marriage
- ¼ of all children live in a home with just one parent, called [3] .... or lone-parent families
- 1 in [4] .... children live in a family with a step-parent and about 65,000 children live with people who are paid to look after them
- increasing numbers of couples decide not to have children or to have them [5] .... in life
- over ½ million old people live in homes for the [6] .... and 12% of British people choose to live alone

3 In your country …

- Who usually lives together in a typical family?
- At what age do children usually move away from home? Why do they do this?
- What age do people mostly get married? How many people stay single?
- How common is it for people to live alone in flats?
- How common is divorce in your country? Where do people live when they are very old?
- What are the main differences you have read about between family life in your country and in the UK?

5.3

The British class system

TYPE OF ACTIVITY

Listening for information and discussion

LEVEL

Advanced

TIME

50–60 minutes

AIMS

To gain an understanding of the class system in British society

VOCABULARY

accent, acknowledge, aspiration, category, class system, contemporary, dialect, essentially, ethnicity, identify with, identity, judge, judgement, observation, outdated, regional, relate to, scholar, social construction, status, stereotype, the media, value

PREPARATION

One photocopy of the worksheet and the audio script for each learner. A set of advanced dictionaries. Option: definition and vocabulary matching exercise.

Warmer

Ask learners what they know about the class system in the UK, and tell them that this is a strong element of British identity. Option: give out a 'word and definition' matching sheet, using vocabulary from the list in the menu. Learners match the vocabulary with the definition. Feed back.

Tell learners that they are going to hear a discussion about class and identity in Britain. Give a copy of the worksheet to each learner and focus them on the introductory activity. In pairs, learners decide which picture typically represents which class and why. Feed back.

> **Answers**
> **a** upper class: in Britain hunting with dogs is associated with upper classes
> **b** middle class: dinner parties, the arts and reading are associated with the middle classes
> **c** working class: casual meal times around a TV, as seen on TV comedy, *The Royle Family*

1 ▶ 25 Focus learners on *The Brighton Festival Debate*. They read through the questions in the grid. Play the audio for learners to complete their responses. Feed back

2 Learners read through the questions and write short responses. Then listen to the audio again, answer the questions and discuss their responses in pairs. Feed back.

> **Answers**
> **1** Evelyn: middle class, author and scholar; people don't always want to talk about class or sometimes even acknowledge it exists; people still judge someone by their accent
> Sophie: (middle) upper class, editor; doesn't agree with Evelyn, class relates to education and doesn't believe class holds people back now
> Ollie: working class, TV presenter; prejudice still exists, class still relates to the history of poverty and inequality of opportunity, and to prejudice
> **2** **1** Multiple identities of wealth, poverty, gender, ethnicity and race, role, (e.g. mother) and class.
> **2** Different regional accents exist in the north and south; in the southern divide the different accents tell us where we've been educated.
> **3** RP isn't Standard English – it's spoken by only 2%. She questions what Standard English is.
> **4** People make assumptions about their background and abilities; a lot of judgments are made about people's social status.
> **3** **1** *Students' own answers.*
> **2** upper class: *one can hear* (you can hear); *ya* (yes) working class: *it ain't' gonna rain, love* (it isn't going to rain, my dear); *'cos* (because) middle and working class: yeah (yes)
> **3** *erm, um, an', uh, well, now, but*

3 Give out copies of the script. Learners complete the information searches. Go over the answers with the class. Highlight the 'clipped' form of spoken English (consonant clusters, glottal stops, etc. in Ollie's English). Compare this with the longer, rounder vowels of Sophie's accent and Evelyn's 'flatter' accent. Play parts of the audio again, as required.

Focus on *Prejudice or fact?* Learners work in small groups. They read the comments on the class system together and discuss their implications. Go over their responses with the class.

Extension

Learners discuss in groups the following questions. *How is society structured in your country? Prompt with class, caste, age, religious commitment, money, success, etc. How do the social groups in your country differ to those of the UK? Who (or what groups) do you mostly identify with?*

Look at the three photos below. Which would you describe as representing the following?

- the working class
- the middle class
- the upper class

The Brighton Festival Debate

1 Listen to the audio and complete the table below.

	Evelyn	Sophie	Ollie
Social group/background			
Work			
Opinions about class			

2 Listen again and answer the following questions.

1 What identities does Evelyn suggest we have?

2 What is the 'North-South divide' that Sophie mentions?

3 What comment does Evelyn make about RP and 'Standard' English?

4 What are the problems Ollie speaks about in categorising people?

3 **English language features**

1 Read the script of the audio and underline new vocabulary and expressions.

2 Find examples of grammar different from Standard English. Which class are they associated with?

3 Mark any communication devices used in spoken, rather than in written, English, e.g. *er …*

Prejudice or fact? The British class system

1 There are constant debates in modern Britain about the relevance of exploring class division. Below are some comments on class. Do you think they are true or false?

- The upper class has a much easier life than other people.
- A middle-class accent, Standard English, is the best.
- Working-class people are less polite and well spoken than other classes.
- People educated at public schools are cleverer than the rest of the population.
- 'I know a person's class as soon as they open their mouth and speak.'

2 Discuss the following questions in your groups.

- To what extent are such statements interesting, factual or just prejudiced?
- What are the problems of expressing stereotypical statements?
- How important is class in your country? How does it affect every day life?
- What is your view of the class system found in Britain?
- Discuss this approach to class and its implications.

6.1

What's on the menu?

TYPE OF ACTIVITY
Listening and matching activity

LEVEL
Elementary to Pre-intermediate

TIME
50–60 minutes

AIMS
To find out about different food in the UK

VOCABULARY
ale, chips, chutney, cod, cooked breakfast, cream tea, custard, fairy cake, inn, lamb, mushy peas, onion rings, pie, pudding, roast dinner, salmon, sherry, steak, steamed, tart, treacle, trifle, try, vegetarian, Caerphilly, Cheddar, Cornish pasty, Ploughman's lunch, Queen of Puddings, Saveloy, Stilton, Victoria sponge cake

PREPARATION
One photocopy of the worksheet for each learner. Pictures of typical British food, if available.

Warmer

Ask learners what they know about British food and typical dishes in the UK (e.g. roast dinner, fish and chips, full breakfast) or show them some pictures of typical British dishes, elicit their names and write responses on the board.

1   Give a copy of the worksheet to each learner. Focus learners on the introductory reading. Tell learners that they are going to find out about different kinds of foods found in Britain and typical places where people eat out. Learners read the letter and answer the questions in pairs. Go over their responses and discuss answers.

> **Answers**
> **1**   many types of foreign restaurants, e.g. Thai, Chinese, Indian, as well as British
> **2**   full English breakfast, fish and chips, lots of puddings
> **3**   a Sunday roast dinner

2   ▶ 26–29   Ask learners if they know of any other popular foreign restaurants in the UK (Italian, Chinese, Arabic, American). Focus them on the visuals of the four restaurants. Learners work in pairs to guess the names of the restaurants by clues in the pictures. Play the audio to see if they were correct. Learners write in the names of the restaurants. Play the audio again for comprehension and pronunciation work.

> **Answers**
> **1**   **1** The Anchor   **2** Bob's Café   **3** 18th Century Tea Rooms   **4** Tall Trees Restaurant
> **2**   **1** D   **2** B   **3** A   **4** C

3   Learners read through the menus and discuss what they think about the food (e.g nice to eat, strange) or if anyone has ever tried these dishes. In pairs, learners choose two places where they would like to eat and what they would try.

4   ▶ 30–32   Tell learners they are now going to find out what some of the dishes are made with. Focus on the listening gap fill. Learners work in pairs to read the text and guess any of the missing words. Play Track 30. Learners complete the gap fill and check their answers together. Repeat the same procedure for Track 31 and 32. Learners then listen again to the complete audio, as required. Go over the answers with the class.

> **Answers**
> **English breakfast**   bacon, beans, potatoes, coffee, juice
> **Ploughman's lunch**   bread, cheese, onion, apple, cucumber
> **Pudding**   cakes, cream, sweet, fruit

Extension

If possible, find some recipes and, if the facilities are available, look up the recipes on the Internet and make some of the dishes. Bring them in to try together. Alternatively, look up the recipes on the internet and study the language and vocabulary of cooking. Learners could also put together their own menu for a British or international restaurant.

1 Read part of a letter from an American girl to her friends. She's on holiday in the United Kingdom and is telling them about the food she has had here.

1 What kinds of restaurants can you find in the UK?

2 What food do British people like to eat?

3 What pub food did she try?

2 Listen to the audio.

1 Write the name of the restaurant or café under the pictures below.

2 Match the place to eat 1–4 with its menu A–D.

3 Choose two places you'd like to eat at and what you'd like to try.

Hello Sue and Ivor,

Well, we've been in the UK for a few weeks and tried a lot of different food. There are restaurants from all over the world here - really good Indian, Thai, and Chinese restaurants - but British food is good too. Yesterday we had a full English breakfast and it was very tasty! British people often eat this at the weekend. We also had a lovely Sunday roast in a pub last week. British people eat lots of delicious puddings, and cakes and fish and chips, of course

1 .... 2 .... 3 .... 4 ....

A ....

18th Century Tea Rooms

Cream tea: 2 scones with strawberry jam & cream	£4.50
Homemade cakes: Victoria sponge, carrot cake, fairy cakes	£2.75
Strawberries and clotted cream	£2.50
Toasted tea cakes and crumpets	£1.20
A selection of sandwiches	£2.75

B ....

Bob's Café

Cod, chips and peas	£6.50
Chicken, chips and peas	£6.50
Saveloy, chips and beans	£4.50
Cornish pasty chips / salad	£4.50
All Day English Breakfast	£4.00
Sides: mushy peas, onion rings	75p

C ....

TALL TREES

Main courses	
Roast leg of Welsh lamb	£12.00
Hereford roast beef in red wine	£15.50
Scottish salmon with new potatoes	£9.50
Desserts	
Sherry trifle	£5.50
Treacle tart and ice cream	£4.50
Queen of puddings	£5.50

D ....

∼∼∼∼ Anchor Menu ∼∼∼∼

Honey roast ham with new potatoes and fresh veg.	£8.50
Steak and ale pie with vegetables.	£10.00
Ploughman's lunch: Stilton, Cheddar or Caerphilly	£6.50
Fish and chips with side salad	£7.50
Vegetarian option: Cheese pie and salad	£6.50

4 Listen to the chef talking about the dishes and fill in the gaps below.

Breakfast

English breakfast: Eggs, b_ _ _n, sausage, mushrooms, b_ _ns, tomatoes, fried p_ _ _ _ _ _s and toast, served with tea or c_ _ _ _e & orange j_ _ _e.

Main meal

Ploughman's lunch: White or brown roll or fresh b_ _ _d, a piece of c_ _ _ _e, tomato, a pickled o_ _ _n, an a_ _ _e, some lettuce, some c_ _ _ber and chutney.

Pudding: Fruit trifle, sponge c_ _ _s, jam, vanilla custard, c_ _ _m, almonds, s_ _ _ _t sherry or liqueur and fresh f_ _ _t.

6.2

The story of British food

TYPE OF ACTIVITY
Listening for information and discussion

LEVEL
Intermediate

TIME
50–60 minutes

AIMS
To gain an awareness of British regional food

VOCABULARY
boil, celebrity chef, crumble, diet, dull, farmers' market, gruel, pasty, powdered, organic, ration, scone, seaweed, speciality, stew, struggle, tasteless, vineyard

PREPARATION
One photocopy of the worksheet and of the audio script for each learner. Display pictures of different dishes from different British countries.

Warmer

Ask learners what kind of food and drink they can think of that is typical of the UK, e.g. fish and chips, a roast dinner, steak and kidney pie, trifle, assorted fruit crumbles and puddings, beer, cider, tea, whisky. Write their responses on the board. Alternatively, write the names of the four countries of the UK on the board. Ask learners to think of some typical dishes (or food and drink) that come from each individual country.

Tell learners they are going to hear a radio programme on food in Britain. A presenter will be talking about food and will interview an expert on popular regional dishes. Pre-teach key vocabulary from the audio. Give out one copy of the worksheet to each learner. This activity can be delivered in two ways.

▶ 33

Option 1 (suitable for stronger learners)
Divide the class into two groups A and B. Tell learners to fold their worksheet in half. One group works with Part A and the other Part B. Working in pairs, learners read through their texts without looking at the other part and try to guess the missing words. Play the audio while they fill in the gaps. Learners then check their answers with their partners. Play the audio again for learners to compete the gap fill. They then read through the other section of the listening (A or B). In pairs, they form the questions required to complete the other text. Learners form new A/B pairs. They ask each other questions to complete the gaps. Go over answers with the class.

Option 2 (suitable for less strong learners)
Learners work in pairs. Learners read through the text and guess the missing words (1–18). Tell one learner to complete Part A of the gap fill and the other Part B. Play the listening while learners fill in the gaps. Learners share their answers together and complete both sections as far as possible. Play the audio again. This time learners check both sections. Go over answers with the class.

> **Answers**
> **Part A**
> **1** meat **3** diet **5** arrived **7** regional **9** cream **11** sausage **13** oats **15** produce **17** banana
> **Part B**
> **2** disease **4** continental **6** dishes **8** miners **10** haggis **12** London **14** fried **16** fruit **18** vineyards

Look at the photos and ask learners to match them with the names of the food in the texts. Learners discuss the information they have read and compare these dishes with typical dishes from their countries; ask what the similarities and differences are. They then search the worksheet to find which countries they are from. Go over answers with the class. Look at the fact file on the worksheet for learners to find any surprises or points to discuss.

> **Picture answers**
> **a** Wales: cheeses **b** England: Banoffee pie **c** Northern Ireland: dulse (fried seaweed) **d** Scotland: haggis

Extension

Give out copies of the script and look in detail at some of the dishes for learners to fill in the lists of food from the four countries of the UK. They can go online and research the different foods, or check them in travel guides if available and present their findings to the class.

Part A

Listen to the audio and fill in the gaps.

The story of British food!

In the 19th century people often lived on poor quality **1** .... and vegetables.

Rationing in the 2nd World War meant people just got used to a bland, tasteless **3** ....

Herbs and spices **5** .... and vegetarian food became popular.

What do you think are the **7** .... food highlights?

It's scones with clotted **9** .... and jam and a cup of tea.

From the north of England you've got Cumberland **11** ....

Bara lawr is a Welsh speciality made of seaweed and **13** ....

Many regions in Britain **15** .... fantastic cheeses.

Banoffee pie is made from a **17** .... and toffee mix on a biscuit base.

Part B

Listen to the audio and fill in the gaps.

The story of British food!

Food was boiled down into thin stews to prevent **2** .... and to hide the taste of unpleasant, old ingredients.

In the 60s and 70s exciting imports of **4** .... foods arrived in greengrocers.

Some new curry **6** .... even originate here.

Cornish pasties were first made for the tin **8** .... down the mines.

In Scotland there's **10** .... and venison, Scotch Broth and Cock-a-leekie soup.

Pie and mash come from **12** ....

In Northern Ireland there's Dulse, which is . **14** .... seaweed.

There are different kinds of British puddings from sherry trifles and **16** .... crumbles.

Britain also has over 300 **18** .... and produces much of its wine for export.

a .... b .... c .... d ....

Factfile

- There are estimated to be 4 million vegetarians in the UK – or between 5–10% of the population.

- The oldest pub in England might be *The Eagle and Lamb* in Stow, *Ye Olde Trip to Jerusalem* in Nottingham or *Ye Olde Fighting Cocks* in St Albans, dating from around 850–1100 AD.

- Borough Market is a famous old London market, dating from before 1014.

- Farmers' markets sell organic vegetables, cheeses, foods and drinks. They are not just a rural thing – there are almost 20 in London.

- The protected geographical status of Stilton, a famous blue cheese, means it cannot come from the village Stilton.

6.3

TYPE OF ACTIVITY
Reading for information and discussion

LEVEL
Advanced

TIME
50–60 minutes

AIMS
To explore controversial aspects of modern British food

VOCABULARY
addiction, a disgrace, animal welfare, cap, dinner lady, nourish, obesity, outlet, plasma, royalty

PREPARATION
Display pictures of typical British dishes. Make one photocopy of the worksheet for each learner. Option: flip chart paper and pens.

21st-century food in Britain

Warmer

Ask learners what kind of dishes they would expect to find on a menu if dining out in the UK. Ask what they would expect to be served in a British family's home. If any learners have visited Britain (or are studying there), ask them what dishes they have tried. Write their responses on the board. Develop the discussion using the prompt questions below (see *Extension* for further activities on local British food).

What kind of reputation does British food have in the rest of the world? Often poor; British food has been described as having little taste, overcooked vegetables – altogether too bland.

What are the positive aspects of eating in the UK? There are great restaurants and food available from all over the world; farmers' markets and organic food are in abundance; there are a lot of regional dishes and *nouvelle cuisine* (new cookery) is being explored; interest in home cooking has increased in recent years.

Do you know of any well-known dishes or food from the four British countries?
England: Sunday roasts with Yorkshire pudding, fish and chips, full English breakfast, pies, ploughman's lunch, Cornish pasties and fruit crumbles
Scotland: haggis, Scotch broth, Scottish salmon, Cock-a-leekie (chicken and leek soup), bannocks (like thick pancakes), porridge, oatcakes, scones (small risen cakes), Dundee cake, whisky
Wales: Welsh rarebit (pronounced 'rabbit'), laverbread (not bread but seaweed with oatmeal), cawl (a kind of broth), Bara brith (fruit loaf)
Northern Ireland: soda bread, potato bread, Ulster fry, (breakfast), oyster and eel dishes, whiskey

What changes have taken place in British cuisine in recent years? The influence of foods from other countries and cultures, the popularity of TV 'masterchefs' (e.g. Jamie Oliver, Delia Smith, Nigel Slater, Rick Stein, Heston Blumenthal) and food programmes have improved standards, quality and innovation in British cuisine and family cooking.

Tell learners they are going to find out about one aspect of the food scene in the UK. Give out one worksheet to each learner. Option: learners describe and discuss the images on the worksheet after completing the main reading activity.

Focus learners on the article by celebrity chef Jamie Oliver. Learners read through the article. Focus on the reading questions. Working in pairs, learners answer the questions. Go over the answers with the class. Find out what surprises them or what they find interesting or shocking.

> **Answers**
> 1 **a** women who produce and serve school meals **b** a TV programme aiming to improve diets in workplaces **c** a food charity set up by Jamie Oliver
> 2 he says they are addictive and causing a health crisis
> 3 only 4–5,000 dinner ladies have been trained
> 4 takeaway and fast food shops: burger bars, kebab shops, curry and pizza houses
> 5 the poverty of people not sufficiently nourishing their families
> 6 there should be laws limiting the number of burger bars and kebab shops in certain areas
> 7 training for dinner ladies, good cooking equipment, seating facilities in schools

Focus learners on the discussion. Learners work in small groups and discuss their views and opinions on fast food. Go over their responses as a class. Option: with reference to the final question, ask learners to produce a spidergram of solutions on flip chart paper. Discuss each group's solutions with the class.

Extension

Ask learners to look up the British celebrity chefs on the Internet and research their profiles and recipes. Learners could prepare a presentation on typical food and drink in the UK or their own countries.

Let's have a cull of the fast food joints, demands Jamie Oliver

JAMIE Oliver has called for a cap on the number of fast food joints in Britain's towns and cities.

The TV chef told MPs the country was facing a 'profound' health crisis because of our addiction to takeaway food.

He said there should be laws limiting the number of burger bars and kebab shops within a certain area.

Giving evidence to the Commons Health Select Committee, he contrasted the ease of setting up a fast-food shop with the 'rigorous' process of getting an extension to your house. He said: 'In California, there's a new law being passed to cap numbers of fast food outlets. I totally agree with that.'

The TV star said he was not against people having the occasional curry or pizza 'but not five to seven days a week, including school'.

Oliver added: 'In this fifth richest country in the world, there is a new poverty that I have never seen before.

'This isn't about fresh trainers or mobile phones or Sky dishes or plasma TV screens – they've got all that. It is a poverty of being able to nourish their family, in any class.

'It directly runs with the outrageous obesity that is happening now ... and it is getting worse and worse.'

Oliver – whose *School Dinners* and *Ministry Of Food* TV series have seen him campaign for better diets in schools and workplaces – also said the £650 million from the government to improve school dinners was not nearly enough.

At least 10 times that amount – £6.5 billion over six years – was necessary to get decent food in schools, he told MPs.

And he hit out at the slow progress made on training kitchen staff to cook decent food.

He said: 'The most important thing in school dinners is training of dinner ladies, then it's equipment, then it's facilities to actually sit these young people down.

'We've got 125,000 dinner ladies and four or five thousand have been trained. It's a disgrace.'

For the second year running, Oliver has given all the book royalties from *Cook with Jamie* to his restaurant charity, the Fifteen Foundation.

Answer the following questions on the text.

1 What are:

   a dinner ladies?

   b Ministry of Food?

   c Fifteen Foundation?

2 What is Jamie Oliver's concern with takeaway foods?

3 What does Jamie call 'a disgrace?'

4 To what foods does he attribute present British rates of obesity?

5 What is the new 'poverty' he talks about?

6 What expectation does he have from the government?

7 Name three key requirements for feeding school children.

Discuss the following questions in your groups.

- To what extent do you agree with Jamie Oliver's views?

- To what degree do you think diet is related to a poverty of lifestyle?

- How popular is fast food in your country?

- How would you rate the standard of home cooking in your country?

- How do you think this compares with Britain?

- What suggestions would you make to improve the standard and quality of food in the UK and in your own country?

7.1

The British money system

**TYPE OF
ACTIVITY**
Reading, listening
and information
search

LEVEL
Elementary to Pre-
intermediate

TIME
40–50 minutes

AIMS
To find out about
British currency and
banks

VOCABULARY
amount, banknote,
bank statement,
cheque, cheque
book, coin, coinage,
credit card,
currency, debit card,
fiver, monarch,
pence, penny,
pound, quid,
sterling, tenner

PREPARATION
One photocopy of
the worksheet for
each learner. Take in
some real currency
or enlarge the
picture on the
worksheet.

Warmer

Ask learners if they can tell you the name of the currency (notes or coins) used in the UK (the pound/£). In pairs/groups, learners write down words used to talk about money: *a pound, a penny, pence, a banknote, a coin, a cheque, a debit/credit card*. Go over their responses and write key vocabulary on the board. If you have authentic examples or photos of coins and notes, show them to the class. Ask some information questions about them, e.g. *Who is the person on the front of each coin/note? Where can you use this money?* (the UK, Isle of Man and Channel Islands). Tell learners they are going to find out the answers to these questions about money in the UK.

1 Give a worksheet to each learner. Focus learners on the photo and ask them what they are called. Tell learners they are going to read about the British money system. Ask them to cover the text and try to answer the questions before reading. Weaker learners can read the text first and then answer the questions. Learners check answers in pairs. Feed back. Learners then look at some informal names for notes and coins, and work in pairs to do exercise 1, *How much?*, matching the names and the amounts. Go over the answers.

> **Answers**
> **Text**
> 1 c
> 2 the current monarch
> 3 b
> 4 c
> **How much?**
> 1 d 2 a 3 e 4 b 5 c

2 ▶ 34 Learners then do *How to say it …* on pronunciation. Look at the examples and find out how learners would pronounce these. Emphasise the contrasting stress between the pronunciation of 50 ('fifty) and 15 (fif'teen). Play the audio through once for learners to repeat. Play the audio again for further practice. Highlight that we don't usually say *pence* in examples 3, 4, 5 and 7 when the amount is over £1; we usually say *a pound* rather than *one pound* for the exact amount £1, and *a quid* is informal.

3 Focus learners on the third exercise, *Find out!* This gives learners an opportunity to explore and compare the value of the pound and the cost of living in the UK. Ask learners if they know the term *exchange rate*, and see if they know the rate of exchange between sterling and their own currency. Take this information to class if you can.

4 Learners then compare the prices of items from their country with British prices. Option: half the class completes numbers a–e and the other completes f–j. They join together, share their findings and compare.

Extension

Develop the final exercise by asking learners to discuss the differences in the cost of living between countries and how that can affect them. Learners work in pairs and write a short page for their British culture book/blog. Alternatively, learners prepare a wall display about UK money/comparison of prices.

Ask learners if they know how to open an account in the UK. Ask them some information questions, e.g. *What's the difference between a current account and a savings account? What must you do to open a bank account in the UK?*

The currency of the United Kingdom is called *sterling* and the main unit is the *pound*. The current monarch's head is on all coins.

There are 100 pennies, or pence, in one pound. The symbol for the penny is 'p', and is written after the amount, e.g. 75p. When speaking, people mostly say '20 p', not '20 pence' or 'pennies'.

There are four Bank of England banknotes: £50, £20, £10 and £5. There are eight types of coins: £2, £1, 50p, 20p 10p 5p, 2p and 1p.

Northern Ireland and Scotland have their own banknotes and these can be used in most places in the UK. English notes show the monarch's head on the front side and a famous or important person on the back. Elizabeth Fry, for example, is on the back of the £5 note. Scottish and Northern Irish notes include a £100 note.

1 How many pence are there in a pound?
   a 20
   b 50
   c 100

2 Who can you see on all British currency?

3 What is the biggest Bank of England note?
   a £20
   b £50
   c £100

4 Where can you use Scottish banknotes?
   a Only in Scotland
   b Scotland and England
   c Most places in the UK

1 How much?

Below are some common informal names of notes and coins. Match the word on the left with the amount of money.

1	a fiver	a	£0.50
2	50 pence	b	£0.01
3	a quid	c	£10.00
4	one 'p'	d	£5.00
5	a tenner	e	£1.00

2 How to say it ...

Listen to the audio and repeat the amounts.

1 30p
2 99p
3 £1.50
4 £2.15
5 £35.07
6 a tenner
7 £12.99
8 a quid

3 Find out!

1 How much are the amounts below in your own national currency?

a £1.00
b £2.50
c £30.00
d £125.00

4 Compare the cost of the things in Britain with the prices in your own country.

a 80p–£1. 90 small loaf of bread
b £1.75–£2.20 a cup of coffee
c £5.50–£8.50 meal in a cafe
d £20–£60 a pair of jeans
e £500–650 pcm. rent one-bed flat
f £25.00 English class
g £30–60 B&B
h £1.50 box of 6 eggs
i £12,000 a small 4-seater car
j 46p 1st class stamp

7.2

The cost of living

TYPE OF ACTIVITY
Reading comprehension and discussion

LEVEL
Intermediate

TIME
45–60 minutes

AIMS
To explore the cost of living and getting work

VOCABULARY
allowance, average, budget, cost of living, estimate, full-time, job centre, part-time, redundant, retail, sign on, typical, upskill, wage, work out

PREPARATION
Flip chart paper and pens. One photocopy of the worksheet for each learner. Option: display some Jobcentre Plus images and leaflets on seeking work, if available.

Warmer

Tell learners they are going to look at work and the cost of living in the UK. Write *Working in the UK* on the board. Elicit vocabulary related to work from learners. Prompt with the headings *working hours, money and pay, applying for and getting a job, losing your job*. Alternatively, ask learners to produce spidergrams under the title *Work in the UK*, using the headings above. Give out flip chart paper/pens to groups of learners. The completed charts can be put up around the room and reviewed as a group.

1   Give a copy of the worksheet to each learner. Focus on the paragraph about job seeking in Britain. Learners read the information and do the matching activity in pairs. Go over the answers with the class and discuss any issues arising.

2   Read through the paragraph on the cost of living with the class. Ask learners the information questions and discuss their answers.

Answers
1   1   e
    2   d
    3   b
    4   a
    5   c
2   1   They get tax credits.
    2   A place where you can look for work and sign on for job seeker's allowance.
    3   He retrained on a part-time retail management course, studying online and attending an evening class at college.
    4   rent, food and transport

3   Focus learners on *The weekly budget*. Ask them to discuss in pairs what three things they spend the most on every week. Write their responses on the board. Alternatively, ask learners if they know the English expression to describe how expensive it is to live somewhere (*the cost of living*). Ask them what they know about the cost of living in the UK. Learners estimate a weekly budget for a young working person or a student from their country, firstly deciding on an appropriate job, e.g. office worker, call centre assistant, shop assistant or a full-time student. Learners compare and contrast a young person's budget with their list and discuss the questions in groups/pairs.

4   In pairs, learners discuss the process of finding work in their countries. They should find out any differences between their system and the British system and present their findings to the class.

Extension

Learners complete a page on money and work for their British culture book/blog. They could also find the answers to a questionnaire as follows.

1   What do people do in the UK when they are looking for work?
2   What financial help can people get if they lose their job?
3   What should you do in the UK before going to an interview?
4   How many women make up the workforce?
5   What is the youngest age that you can work full-time?
6   At what age do most men/women retire?

For more activities on money/working in the UK, see *ESOL Activities* and *English at Work*.

Job seekers in Britain

When looking for work in Britain people go to the job centre to look for a new job. First you must sign on and then you can get a *Job seeker's* Allowance. This is an amount of money given by the government to help you live while you while you are looking for work.

Matt's story is a typical example of someone's search for work. He spent a lot of time looking for jobs online, in local and national newspapers, in Jobcentre Plus offices and in employment agencies.

He finally found full-time work in a clothing department store. He then decided to *upskill* by doing a part-time retail management course, studying online and going twice a week to an evening class at college. He's now thinking about retraining to become a manager.

The cost of living

In the United Kingdom the cost of living is very high compared to many other countries. London, for example, is around the 5th most expensive city in the world. Living expenses such as *rent*, food and transport are also very high compared to most people's wages.

There are ways to help reduce *tax* paid by people with families or who are sick. These are called 'tax credits'. Local councils also offer people reduced council tax payments and other forms of *income* support.

1 Match the words with their meanings.

1 to upskill
2 an income
3 a job seeker
4 a tax
5 rent

a payment to the government
b a person looking for work
c money you pay to live somewhere
d the money a person earns
e to get more training

2 Answer the following questions.

1 What help do families get with tax payments?
2 What is Jobcentre Plus?
3 What did the young man do to improve his job opportunities?
4 Which living expenses are high in Britain?

The weekly budget

Here is a list of how much money a typical young working person might spend each week.

3 Read through the budget.

1 In pairs discuss what items are essential and what are luxuries.

2 Write down a typical weekly budget for a young working person in your country.

- Which items are the same? Which are different?

- Which costs are similar? Which are different?

- What changes would you suggest to reduce his/her spending?

Weekly budget	
rent:	£130
utilities (gas, electricity, water):	approx £12
telephone:	£15
council tax:	£12
bus fares:	£15
food:	£40
clothing / hair: approx	£12–15
gym:	£12.50
drink / going out: approx	£25.00–£35
other:	£10
savings:	£10
Total expenses:	£295
Weekly income after tax:	£305

4 Compare the process of looking for work, unemployment and retraining in Britain with that of your own country.

7.3

High finance

TYPE OF ACTIVITY
Reading for information and discussion

LEVEL
Advanced

TIME
50–60 minutes

AIMS
To gain an understanding of economic issues with in the UK

VOCABULARY
bonus, distribution of wealth, economy, equitable, finance, financial markets, get a foot on the ladder, life expectancy, minimum wage, standard of living, tax credits, the housing ladder, the poverty line, FTSE, GDP

PREPARATION
One set of cards for each group of three/ four learners. Dictionaries. Option: enlarge the worksheet if possible.

Warmer

Tell learners they are going to explore aspects of the UK's financial sector. Ask them what they know about the British economy and its strengths and weaknesses. Prompt with the following categories: the service industries (finance, tourism, education, retail, etc.); production and other industries (agriculture, manufacturing, construction, mining, etc.). Write their responses on the board.

Learners work in groups of 3–4. Give out sets of the headings A–D. Ask learners to read them and discuss briefly what kind of information the sections may include. Tell them they are now going to read different pieces of information which they have to place under the correct headings.

Give out sets of information cards, turned upside down. Learners spread the cards out. Ask them to pick up one card at a time and discuss its content. They then decide under which heading to put each card. Learners continue to do this until they have completed the four sets of cards. Option: ask learners to sequence the cards in order of the most significance or interesting information. Check that learners have grouped the cards correctly.

Go through each card with the class and discuss its content, checking new vocabulary and expressions, as required. Draw out the key issues to debate and reflect on with the class (child work practices, pay inequalities, importance of London and finance markets to the economy, unequal distribution of land, cost of housing, welfare, poverty and life expectancy). Learners discuss this information and compare it with the situation in their own countries.

Extension

Learners research further the specific information from the worksheet, e.g. the importance of London as a centre of commerce and trade for Britain, the cost of living in the UK, retirement in the UK. This information can be added to their British culture blog/book. Learners could also research similar information for their own countries and report this back to the class. Do an internet search for British broadsheet newspapers such as the *Financial Times*, *The Times*, *The Guardian*, *The Independent* and *The Telegraph*. Search on the BBC Worldwide website for news and topical programmes.

A

The standard of living and the distribution of wealth

It is estimated that a single British person needs a yearly salary of around £15,000 a year before tax to achieve a basic but acceptable standard of living. The wish to have a computer and internet access imposes significant extra costs on low-income households.

In Britain, the standard of living is relatively high compared to many countries but in recent years, increasing numbers of families have found themselves on the poverty line.

There is a 10-year difference in life expectancy in London depending on where you live. It has been claimed that for every underground stop heading east from wealthy Kensington, life expectancy of the inhabitants drops by one year.

Since 1995, the income per week for British workers has gone up by 40% but for the very rich the rise has been 400%, or 4 times as high. In the 1970s, wealth distribution was one of the most equitable in Europe but the gap between rich and poor is again on the increase.

B

The UK economy and the financial markets

Britain has a strong economic position. In 2011 it was the 6th largest economy in the world. The service sector dominates the UK economy, a feature normally associated with a developed country, and makes up about 73% of GDP.

10% of the UK's GDP comes from the financial markets. Earnings and bonuses in the financial world have been attacked as being too high but others argue that 'big players' need big rewards.

London is the world capital for foreign exchange trading. It is also a major legal centre, with four of the six largest law firms in the world headquartered there.

London is a very important financial market. The two centres are the City, or Square Mile, home to the London Stock Exchange (FTSE), and business quarter Canary Wharf. It is the world's most important international business centre, followed by New York and Hong Kong.

C

Work patterns in the UK

Around half the workforce in the UK does non-manual work. In the 70s it was 30%. The shift was due to the decline of industries such as coal, steel and manufacturing, in Wales, the Midlands and northern England and Northern Ireland.

British people are now expected to work longer than ever. Between April 2010 and November 2018, women's retirement ages are increasing to 65. Retirement for men and women at 66 years is coming into effect from 2016.

It is thought that there are two million children at work in the UK at any one time. From age 14, children are allowed to work up to five hours a week in school time and 25 hours in the holidays. The minimum wage applies from age 15 and above.

Women make up 45% of the workforce in the UK. However, the average hourly rate of pay is about 20% lower than that of men. In 2010 rates for men were £13 for full-timers, £7.69 for part-timers. For women, hourly rates were £11.68 for full-timers, £8 for part-timers.

D

The cost of living and the tax system in the UK

Taxable income starts for a single person from around £8,000 though this may be raised to £10,000. People with families on low level incomes can apply for tax credits, income support and other benefits to help them.

Typical weekly costs in 2011 were: food and drink £48; clothing £6.50; housing £84; household goods and services £20; personal goods, services and health £6; transport £17; social and cultural activities £30. Total expenditure £212 per week.

In the UK, the top rate of tax is currently around 40% of a person's income. This compares with a rate of 98% in the 1970s.

In Britain, the cost of an average two-bedroom flat can range from £90–260,000. Since 1970, house prices have increased by about 300% related to the cost of living. Wages have not risen accordingly and first time buyers find it hard to get a foot on the British housing ladder.

8.1

TYPE OF ACTIVITY
Reading and information exchange

LEVEL
Elementary to Pre-intermediate

TIME
40–50 minutes

AIMS
To explore a range of British celebrations

VOCABULARY
adult, bonfire, candle, card, celebrate, decorate, firework, fool, guy, joke, parade, pumpkin

PREPARATION
One copy of the questionnaire for each learner. One set of reading cards per group of six learners. One photocopy of the worksheet for each learner as a handout.

British celebrations

Warmer

Ask learners if they know the names of any British celebrations. Prompt them with images of celebrations for learners to identify, e.g. Guy Fawkes' night, Valentine's Day, Christmas. Alternatively, play 'draw the man' or 'hangman' with words associated with celebration, e.g. *festival, holiday*. Learners guess the letters of the word. For each incorrect letter, draw a section of a stick man up to nine strokes.

Tell learners they're going to read about some famous British celebrations. Give out one copy of the questionnaire to each learner and focus on the headings. Ask learners what questions they need to ask to get the correct information. *What's the name of the celebration? What's the date? What do people do on this day?* Drill the pronunciation of questions. There are two ways to deliver the next stage.

Option 1: small group information exchange (suitable for stronger learners)
Give out one set of cards to groups of six learners. Each reads their own card and fills in the information about their own celebration on their questionnaire. Learners then ask each other questions to complete the rest of the chart. Go over the answers with the class and discuss any points of interest.

Option 2: pair work information search (suitable for weaker learners)
Put enlarged photocopies of each information card onto separate tables or pin them round the room. Tell learners they are going to read about some popular celebrations. Learners work in pairs and walk round the room to complete their questionnaires. Go over the answers with the class. With smaller groups, do this as a class, looking at each celebration card, checking answers and discussing any points of interest.

Answers

1	New Year's Day	1 January	People visit family and friends, have parties and relax.
2	May Day	1 May	Fairs to celebrate the beginning of summer. Maypole dance.
3	Mother's Day	March or April (fourth Sunday in Lent)	People give cards, presents or flowers to their mothers.
4	April Fool's Day	1 April	Children and adults play silly jokes on people and say *April fool!* to anyone who falls for the joke. Newspapers traditionally publish false stories and readers try to find them.
5	Hallowe'en	31 October	People dress in ghostly clothes and have parties.
6	Guy Fawkes' Night	5 November	People light bonfires, burn 'Guys' and watch fireworks.

Finally, if you have images of the celebrations, learners match them with the activity cards. Find out what learners think about these customs and if there are any surprises. Discuss and compare any similarities with the learners' own customs from their own countries, or religious or ethnic group.

Extension

The class make a timeline following the British festival year, adding further celebrations and significant days in the calendar, e.g. historic days (Armistice Day on 11th November; the Queen's official birthday; the Lord Mayor's show; The Edinburgh Military Tattoo); religious celebrations (see Unit 8.2); sports events (London Marathon, the Oxford and Cambridge Boat Race) and about other popular celebrations, e.g. Burns Night; St Patrick's Day; Notting Hill Carnival; Chinese New Year). Learners can do more research into any of these and/or develop their wall chart/book/blog.

1

New Year's Day is on 1st January. It is a national holiday and people often visit their family or friends or just relax. Lots of people also go to parties on the evening of 31st December, known as Hogmanay, and sing a famous song about friendship called *Auld Lang Syne*. There are many street celebrations and house parties.

2

1st May is called May Day. It's a national holiday to celebrate the beginning of spring and summer. It was firstly a pagan festival – now there are fairs and people, usually children, dance round a flowery Maypole. People have celebrated May Day for over 2,000 years.

3

People celebrate Mother's Day in March or April. This falls on the 4th Sunday in Lent, a time just before Easter. On this day people give their mother a card and a present, or flowers. Sometimes they have Sunday lunch together.

4

In Britain there is a funny celebration called April Fool's Day. This is on 1st April and children and adults play silly jokes on each other. For example, the TV may broadcast a funny but untrue story. They can only play these tricks before twelve o'clock midday.

5

Hallowe'en is a ghostly night. People dress in strange clothes and go to Hallowe'en parties in the evening. People also decorate their houses with pumpkins, lit with candles and children go 'trick or treating'. This celebration is on 31st October.

6

On 5th November, people remember the night when a man put a bomb under Parliament in 1604. He was called Guido Fawkes. Bonfire night is also called Guy Fawkes' Night. In the evening people light big bonfires, burn 'Guys', have some food and watch the fireworks.

British celebrations questionnaire

Write the information about your celebration in the correct box below.
Ask others questions about their celebration. Write their answers below.

Celebration	Date	What people do on this day
1		
2		
3		
4		
5		
6		

Religious and non-religious festivals

TYPE OF ACTIVITY
Reading and information exchange

LEVEL
Intermediate

TIME
45–60 minutes

AIMS
To gain awareness of important religious festivals in the UK

VOCABULARY
ascend, ascension, affiliation, bun, celebrate, community, cross, enlightenment, established, fairy light, fast, feast, ignorance, joyful, mark, mass, pancake, reflect, sacred, solemn, spice, symbol, toss

PREPARATION
One photocopy of the worksheet for each pair of learners. Display pictures of the celebrations to elicit vocabulary and take in dictionaries.

Warmer

Write *Religious festivals in the UK* on the board. Ask learners what religions are important in the UK and ask for the names of their important celebrations. Write their responses on the board. Tell learners that they are going to look at some important religious and non-religious festivals. Elicit vocabulary about Christmas or Easter, showing them pictures as prompts, e.g. Christmas tree/card, Father Christmas, Easter eggs.

Ask learners if they know which is the biggest religion in the UK. You could either read aloud the paragraph below, or write the religions on the board and ask learners to guess the percentages.

> About 70% of people say they are Christians (10% of Christians are Catholic, but in Northern Ireland 40% are Catholic). Other religions in the country are Muslim (3%) Hindu (1%), Sikh (0.6%), Jewish (0.5%), Buddhist (0.3%), other religions 0.3%. Around 20% of people either belong to no religious group or do not state their religion.

Form A/B pairs. Give one learner Text A and the other Text B. Using the question form *Could you tell me about ...?*, learners take turns to answer their partners' questions about the festivals in their text. Go over the answers with the class and discuss any issues arising.

Focus learners on the crossword puzzle. In pairs they complete the crossword activity. Option: Give out Part A clues across, and the answers to part B, to one student. Give out Part B clues down, and the answers to part A, to the other. Learners exchange clues and answers. Go over answers with the class.

Answers

Across		Down	
3	Wesak	**1**	Easter
5	turkey	**2**	Burns
7	Glastonbury	**4**	Sikhs
8	Christmas	**6**	Notting Hill
9	Boxing	**10**	eggs
11	Edinburgh		
12	public		

Extension

Learners can have a discussion on festivals, as follows:
1 What interests you about the festivals described in the texts?
2 Do you think the religious or non-religious celebrations sound more interesting?
3 Which would you most like to see or go to?
4 What are the most important festivals in your country? (Describe these to your group.) How do you celebrate them?
5 What differences are there in how festivals are celebrated in the UK?

Focus learners on the different word stress patterns on three-syllable words, e.g 'festival (●••); im'portant (•●•); under'neath (••●). Practise pronunciation, finding other examples from the text, e.g. *calendar* /ˈkælɪndəʳ/; *celebrates* /ˈselɪbreɪts/; *believer* /bɪˈliːvəʳ/; *December* /dɪsˈembəʳ/; *including* /ɪnˈkluːdɪŋ/; (note that *chocolate* is pronounced with two syllables: /ˈtʃɒklət/).

Learners research more about religious celebrations in the UK to include in their book/blog. For more information and activities on different religious ceremonies in the UK see *ESOL Activities Entry* 3.

A Christmas is the most important festival in the UK. It celebrates the birth of Jesus Christ. People decorate fir trees and exchange cards and presents. On Christmas Eve (24 December), many people attend midnight mass in church. Christmas Day (25 December) is a public holiday when people usually visit their families and have a traditional lunch together of roast turkey or goose and Christmas pudding.

The next day is called Boxing Day and is also a public holiday. Many people go with their children to funny traditional shows called pantomimes.

Easter (March/April) is the most important date in the church calendar, although people don't celebrate it as much as Christmas. Good Friday is a public holiday that marks Christ's death. During Easter, people eat hot cross buns and chocolate eggs. Forty days before Easter is Shrove Tuesday, also called Pancake Day. Some people give up eating certain things during Lent, which is the period between Shrove Tuesday and Easter.

Other religious celebrations include Id al Fitr, a three-day Muslim holiday, time of prayers and feasting that marks the end of Ramadan, the Islamic holy month of fasting. Diwali is a five-day festival of light, celebrated by Hindus and Sikhs. It marks the victory of knowledge over ignorance. Yom Kippur is the most sacred and solemn day in the Jewish calendar. It's a day to reflect on your actions over the past year. Wesak is the most important Buddhist festival. It celebrates the Buddha's birthday, enlightenment and death.

B There are a lot of festivals and celebrations that aren't religious. During the summer months in particular there are festivals dedicated to arts and culture. The Edinburgh Festival in August celebrates theatre and comedy, The National Eisteddfod is a celebration of the Welsh language, literature and music while Glastonbury is the UK's most famous rock and pop music festival, where stars from around the globe attract huge audiences.

Over the last 50 years, more and more festivals have been started to celebrate different groups in society. In August, thousands of people go the Notting Hill area of London to drink, eat, dance and watch the Carnival parade. It began as a celebration of Caribbean culture after racial violence in the 1950s and now celebrates racial diversity in general. Similarly there are Gay Pride parades across the country. The biggest party is in Soho, London in July.

There are also events which are celebrated by certain national groups. The Irish celebrate St Patrick's Day on 17 March. On 26 January, Burns' Night, the Scots remember their national poet, Robert Burns. Haggis and whisky are almost compulsory! The Chinese New Year is the most important celebration for the Chinese community and time is spent with family and friends. 'Chinatowns' in various cities come alive with lanterns, dragons and Chinese food stalls. If you ever go to one of these events, you'll see all kinds of people there just to have a good time!

Ask your partner about:

Burns' Night   St Patrick's Day   Glastonbury
National Eisteddfod   Gay Pride   Notting Hill

Ask your partner about:

Id al Fitr   Boxing Day   Good Friday
Yom Kippur   Wesak   Diwali

A Clues across

3   The most important Buddhist festival (5)

5   Traditionally, people eat this bird on Christmas Day (6)

7   a three-day music festival (11)

8   25th December (9)

9   After Christmas comes .... Day (6)

11   Scottish city with arts festival (9)

12   Good Friday is a .... holiday (6)

B Clues down

1   Festival in March or April (6)

2   A famous Scottish poet (5)

4   Diwali is celebrated by Hindus and .... (5)

6   Carnival in London to celebrate London's ethnic mix (7,4)

10   Children are given Easter .... (4)

8.3

Attitudes and values

TYPE OF ACTIVITY
Reading, gap fill and discussion

LEVEL
Advanced

TIME
50–60 minutes

AIMS
To gain an understanding of British attitudes and values

VOCABULARY
attitude, breeding, characteristic, eccentric, fair play, flirt, flush, grimly, pay tribute to, personify, privacy, prune, rile, tinker, tut, underdog, unprecedented, valour, value

PREPARATION
One copy of the worksheet for each learner. Advanced dictionaries. Display pictures of people in queues, doing gardening, on allotments, dressed up for a fun run / medieval pageant, on the underground

Warmer

Tell learners that they're going to look at some different ideas of British values. Write *attitudes and values* on the board. Learners discuss the words in pairs/groups and give definitions. (*attitude*: the way a person thinks, feels and behaves; *values*: the moral principles and beliefs that a person or group think are important.) Ask them what they believe to be the typical characteristics of British people. (possible responses: *insular, tolerant, reserved, conservative, polite, sense of humour*.) Then ask what are the typical attitudes and values of British people. (possible responses: *freedom of speech, democracy, tradition, fair play*)

1   Give a copy of the worksheet to each learner. Learners read the text and complete the gap fill in pairs using dictionaries. Check the answers as a class.

2   Focus on exercise 2. Learners answer the comprehension questions and check in pairs. Go over the answers with the class.

> **Answers**
> **1** **1** breeding **2** tinkering **3** tuts **4** grief **5** rants **6** riled **7** flirtation
> **8** psyche **9** discomfort **10** valour
> **2** **1** when walking their dogs and pruning the garden hedge
> **2** by joking, getting flushed and saying they're going to write a letter
> **3** by supporting the underdog and saying a team has lost with valour or lost well
> **4** eye-rolls, head shakes, tuts and sighs
> **5** a love affair with DIY, attitude towards sex, preference for animals to children, attitude to sport

3   Ask learners how much they think the article is based on true observation and how much is probably fiction. Develop a discussion around the key points of the article. Draw out any issues related to contradictory values and strange attitudes. Find out what people's views are on these. Ask them which attitudes and values are similar to/different from their country. Discuss their understanding of the following statements.
Societies change over time but their reputations lag behind.
The British are the only people on the planet obsessed with being sorry.
An Englishman's home is his castle.

4   Focus learners on the three newspaper headlines and ask them to predict what they'll be about. Learners read the short articles and discuss what they reveal about British attitudes, values and beliefs. Learners compare values and attitudes within their own countries.

Extension

Learners research aspects of British values and beliefs and report back their findings to the class. They can research texts online, and books for further reading. Interesting films include: *Secrets and Lies, West is West, My Beautiful Launderette, Goodbye Mr. Chips, Brief Encounter*.

The text takes a humorous look at attitudes and values in modern Britain.

1 Fill the gaps in the text using the words below.

breeding   discomfort   flirtation   grief   psyche   rants   riled   tinkering   tuts   valour

---

British people display a confusing range of contradictions in their values and attitudes. The shy and socially reserved British have no hesitation in going up to strangers and asking deeply personal questions about age, sex and [1]_____ – as long as it's about their dog.

Walking the dog is about the greatest invitation for conversation the British can come up with, next to a chat while pruning the front garden hedge. Then the privacy barrier is again raised by the deeply inhibited British – though mostly by women, as their men are happier spending their free time '[2]_____' in their garden sheds!

The British expect each other – and foreigners – to observe the rules, especially the rule of queuing. Even a Martian dropped from another planet would get eye-rolls, head shakes, [3]_____ and sighs, if it dared to queue-jump. When Princess Diana died, the press commented on the 'unprecedented public display of emotion and [4]_____'. However one wry commentator added that the British paid tribute to Diana by doing what they do best: queuing – for flowers, to sign books and pay their last respects.

In typical British fashion, anger is channelled into jokes and ritual (and preferably humorous) [5]_____ – about the weather, the government, the price of petrol. But you know when a British person is really [6]_____ because they get flushed, then swear they're going to write a letter!

With all this inhibition and repression of emotion, a healthy outlet for non-conformity is expressed by their love and respect for 'the eccentric' – as long as they don't have to live next door to them.

Along with a national obsession for 'the amateur' personified in the British love affair with DIY, a childish embarrassment about sex and [7]_____ that makes the French laugh, a little disguised preference for animals over children, there's also their ambivalent attitude to sport.

Fair play resonates deeply in the British [8]_____, and support for the 'underdog' is an ideal which the British cling to, mixed with a self-punishing mourning and much head shaking at its loss. When top sports people talk about playing to win and 'game plans' people agree but there's a nervous [9]_____ deep in the heart of the British, saying this isn't really what they should approve of. To people's great relief, the British team may have lost 'with [10]_____' and the most important comment, grimly but cheerfully spoken, is – didn't they lose well!

---

2 Answer the following questions about the article.

1 When do British people like to start conversations?

2 In which ways do people express their anger?

3 How do British people express their sense of fair play?

4 How do British people react to breaking the queuing rule?

5 What behaviour does the writer find amusing?

3 How much do you think the article is based on true observation of attitudes, and how much is most likely fiction?

4 Read the headlines A–C and discuss what you think they show about British values and attitudes.

A

Cross at work

A woman was asked to remove her necklace and crucifix at work because it was not thought appropriate for an air hostess. Sarah Jay, from Sheffield, said, "I was shocked! My friend Maryam wears a veil to work and no one's complained about that!"

B

A dog's life

Millionaire Mrs Annabelle West, 89, left her pet poodle Minnie her house and over half a million pounds in her will, it was revealed. Payments will cover a dog walker and feeder for the rest of its life.

C

Gay couple win case over hotel ban

A court has ordered that a bed and breakfast compensate a gay couple after being refused a room. The two men were awarded £1,800 each.

British history chart

TYPE OF ACTIVITY
Reading and matching activity

LEVEL
Elementary to Pre-intermediate

TIME
40–50 minutes

AIMS
To find out about key periods in British history

VOCABULARY
bridge, build, castle, cathedral, conquer, heritage, historic, invade, religion, ship, skyscraper, stone, tribe, wall, Anglo-Saxon, AD (Anno Domini = after Christ's birth), BC (before Christ), HMS, The Industrial Revolution, Parliament, the Romans, Viking

PREPARATION
One photocopy of the worksheet for each group of four learners.

Warmer

Ask learners what they know about British history. Find out about any important dates, events or people that they know. Write any key answers on the board, e.g.
English Civil War in 1600s: Oliver Cromwell and King Charles I
Industrial Revolution; the British Empire: Queen Victoria
First World War 1914–18
Second World War 1939–45: Churchill

Tell learners they're going to find out about some important places in British history. Give a copy of the worksheet to each group of four learners and focus on the pictures. Find out if they know the names of any of the places. Focus on exercise 1. Ask learners to look at the titles above each box and complete the titles (clues are in the names, e.g. *stone, wall, castle, cathedral, ship*). Go over answers with the class. They should ignore the gaps (a–i) until exercise 2. Note that the answer to gap 1 is one word.

Answers			
1		**2**	
1 Stone		**a** five	
2 Wall		**b** Scotland	
3 Tower		**c** battle	
4 Castle		**d** Welsh	
5 Cathedral		**e** Fire	
6 HMS		**f** Lord	
7 Bridge		**g** railway	
8 buildings		**h** assembly	
9 skyscraper		**i** business	

2   Focus on the readings under the pictures and the vocabulary for exercise 2. Learners work in pairs and read the paragraphs, choosing the correct missing word or number. Go over the answers with the class.

Check comprehension by asking some information questions about the texts, e.g. *When was Stonehenge built? Why was Hadrian's Wall built?* Alternatively, make a questionnaire on the texts for them to answer.

3   With the class, find out where each building or structure fits on the timeline. Learners write these on the line. Discuss any points arising with the class.

Look again at the pictures on the chart and the timeline. Ask them to imagine the kind of life people had at this time in Britain, e.g. *What did people eat/wear? What did they live in? Where did they live? Did they hunt, farm or both? Did they have medicine? Did they use electricity, fire, candles?* Learners can look up images of life in the UK at these times on the Internet.

Extension

Learners continue to develop a wall chart, book or blog using these, or other images and information from the Internet or books. Also a group or class discussion on the importance of history is interesting here. Learners can talk about the following questions: Why is the history of a country important? What can we learn from history? What people are famous in the history of your country? What places in history are important in your country? How did people live at this time?

1 .... henge

These ancient stones were put up in south west England around
a ....
thousand years ago. Some people think they're a kind of calendar. It is an important religious place for the Druids.

2 Hadrian's ....

This wall was built around 122 AD by the Roman Emperor Hadrian between what is now England and
b .... It formed the northern border of the Roman Empire. It's 73 miles long and runs from the east to the west coast.

3 The .... of London

In 1066, William Duke of Normandy in France won a great c ....
and took over England. He started to build the Tower of London to control the local people. The White Tower was completed in 1100.

6 .... Victory

This famous ship was in a great battle in 1805. The captain, f ....
Nelson is famous because he defeated Napoleon's navy at Trafalgar, but he died on the HMS Victory.

5 St Paul's

In 1666 the Great
e .... of London destroyed a lot of the city, including St Paul's Cathedral. King Charles II ordered a new cathedral which was built by Christopher Wren. At this time the British Empire began to grow in America and India.

4 Caernarfon

This huge castle was built between 1283 and 1330. Edward I built a lot of castles around Wales, to keep control of the
d .... after the last Welsh prince, Llewelyn the Last, was killed in 1282.

7 The Forth Rail

A great bridge was opened in 1890 to carry a
g .... across the river Forth from Edinburgh to the north. In the Industrial Revolution, there were a lot of changes in the country and many new things were invented.

8 Stormont

Parliament building, Stormont, opened in 1932. This is part of a group of buildings where the Northern Ireland
h .... meets.

9 The 'Gherkin'

This building is a skyscraper in the
i .... centre of London. It opened in 2004 and is an iconic office block in the city. Londoners gave it the nickname 'Gherkin' because of its shape.

1 Fill in the place names on the chart

2 Put the words below in the correct gaps.

Welsh   assembly   Scotland   business   railway   five   Lord   battle   Fire

3 Write in the places and objects in the photos on the timeline below.

History timeline

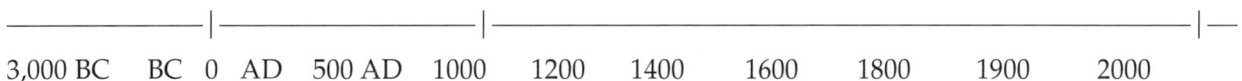

3,000 BC   BC   0   AD   500 AD   1000   1200   1400   1600   1800   1900   2000

9.2

**TYPE OF
ACTIVITY**
Reading, listening
and information
search

LEVEL
Intermediate

TIME
45–60 minutes

AIMS
To find out about
the history of the
four countries of the
United Kingdom

VOCABULARY
arrival, battle,
bronze, cape,
chessman, conquer,
defeat, heir, helmet,
high cross, invade,
ivory, medieval,
nugget, pagan, rule,
shore, symbolise,
tiny, tribe, via,
walrus

PREPARATION
Worksheet cut into
four sections, one
set for each pair or
group. Display a
map of Europe.
Option 1: prepare
date cards, using
the dates from
cards A–D.

A date with British history

Warmer

Ask learners what they know about the history of the UK and its four countries. As background, read out the information below. A map of Europe is useful here. Ask learners if they have any questions.

> Through the centuries, the British Isles have been invaded by many different tribes, from northern, central and southern Europe. Many groups settled and mixed with the existing population. These included the Celts, arriving from Europe around 500BC and the Romans, who ruled for 400 years, first coming to England in 55BC.
> Later the Nordic Vikings ruled in the north and east of Britain while the Anglo-Saxons held the south and the west.
>
> In 1066 the Normans invaded from France and won a great battle against the Anglo-Saxon king Harold. Britain has not been overrun since this time. However, in the Battle of Britain in 1940, in the Second World War, Hitler's air force was narrowly beaten. This helped prevent the German invasion in 1940, though bombing raids continued throughout the War.

1   Tell learners they're going to hear stories about four objects which are important in our understanding of the early history of the British Isles. Give out the top part of the worksheet. In pairs, learners discuss what they think the objects are and how old they might be.

2   ▶ 35–38 Play the audio for learners to write down the place, country and date of the object and check their answers together. Listen again, go over their answers and deal with any points arising.

> **Answers**
>
> 1   **a**   Mold Gold Cape: the village of Mold, Wales, 3–4 thousand years ago.
>   **b**   Sutton Hoo helmet: Sutton Hoo ship grave in Suffolk, England, 7th century
>   **c**   Lewis Chessmen: Isle of Lewis, Scotland, 12th century
>   **d**   High Cross: Ardboe, Northern Ireland, 8–9th century

3   Tell learners they're now going to find out more of the history of the four individual countries and the UK.

Option 1: information exchange – dates

Learners work in groups of four. Give each student a card A–D. Place the date cards that you have prepared in a pile on the table. Learners pick a date and find out what happened at this time. Alternatively, write the dates on the board and learners take turns to choose a date. They look for the information on their card for their group to write down (spelling out difficult names). Go over the information and vocabulary with the class.

Option 2: sorting

Remove the titles from each card A–D. Give a set of cards to each pair/group of learners. They read the cards and decide which card is English, (Northern) Irish, Scottish and Welsh history. To make this more challenging, cut the sentences up individually for pairs/groups to categorise. Go over the answers with the class.

Learners then pick which five dates they think are the most important or interesting. They present these to the class, explain why they've chosen them and can research the dates to follow up in subsequent lessons.

Extension

Give learners the following dates and periods for general UK history: 1300s (black death); 1707 (Act of Union); 1800s (Industrial Revolution); 1914 and 1939 (world wars); 1973 (European Union). Learners research these dates and report back to the class on their significance. Refer them to the British Museum website at http://www.britishmuseum.org/, or they can do their own research. They could set up 'interviews' with people of the time, witnessing different events, e.g. the arrival of St Patrick in Ireland, the Norman conquest.

Ancient history

1 **Look at the pictures and match the words below with the pictures.**

a cape   a chessman   a helmet   a high cross

A	**B**	**C**	**D**
Place:	Place:	Place:	Place: ....
Country:	Country:	Country:	Country: ....
Date:	Date:	Date:	Date: ....

2 **Listen to the audio and fill in the information about the objects above.**

A Irish history

432AD St Patrick went to Ireland to spread Christianity and convert the Irish.

1169 The beginning of over 800 years of occupation of Ireland by English rulers.

1500s Rebellion followed by repression of the Irish by English rulers for the next 300 years.

1921 After a War of Independence, Ireland was divided into Protestant north and Catholic south. This started years of fighting in Northern Ireland.

1998 Power sharing between Protestants and Catholics was agreed and the Northern Irish Assembly opened.

2007 After stopping for five years, the Assembly sat again.

B Welsh history

4000BC Farming tribes lived in the valleys of Wales.

800s The Welsh tribes joined together to fight Viking invaders but needed English help.

1277 Edward I of England invaded and took control. Llwelyn the Last was defeated.

1400s Owain Glyndwr of Wales fought against the English rulers but he was defeated.

1999 The Welsh Assembly was set up with limited powers.

2011 Welsh people voted for more power to make their own laws.

C Scottish history

400 The Scotti people from Ireland invaded the land now known as Scotland.

800 The early kings of Scotland were crowned on the Stone of Destiny at Scone, near Perth.

1296 Edward 1 tried to invade Scotland. He was not successful but did take the Stone of Destiny from Scone to Westminster Abbey in London where it remains today.

1603 James VI of Scotland was crowned king of England too after Queen Elizabeth left no heir.

1700s The Jacobites tried to reinstate the Catholic monarchy in Britain. Bonnie Prince Charlie led an invasion of England in 1745 but failed.

1999 Scotland's Parliament was reinstated with limited powers.

D English history

43AD The Romans invaded and finally took control of the southern part of Britain.

122 The Romans built Hadrian's wall to form the northern border of the Roman Empire.

1066 William of Normandy invaded England and killed Harold, the Anglo-Saxon king.

1296 King Edward 1 of England invaded Scotland but was not successful.

1509-1547 Henry VIII's reign saw the union of England and Wales and separation from the Roman Catholic Church.

1642 The English Civil War began. England had no king for 11 years after Charles I was executed in 1649.

People who changed British history

TYPE OF ACTIVITY
Listening, information search and debate

LEVEL
Advanced

TIME
50–60 minutes

AIMS
To gain an understanding of important individuals in British history

VOCABULARY
aristocratic, hot air balloon, impact, influence

PREPARATION
One photocopy of the worksheet for each learner.
Display pictures of famous or important British historical figures.

Warmer

Ask learners if they can think of famous British 'history makers' (either internationally or within the UK). Write their names up on the board. Elicit from the whole group what kind of information they'd like to know about them. Write up some of these questions on the board, e.g. *When was this person born? What special thing(s) are they remembered for? What impact did this have on the UK or the world at large?* Prompt with a picture of a well-known British person, if required, e.g. *He published 'On the Origin of Species' outlining his theory of evolution in 1859* (Darwin); *She ruled over the British Empire from 1837* (Queen Victoria).

▶ 39–40 Give out one copy of the worksheet to each learner. Focus learners on the introductory paragraph. Ask them what makes a person a 'history maker' (possible answers include: *scientific discovery, medical advancement, political change, revolution, war, writing, philosophy, leadership, exploration*). Write their responses on the board.

Tell learners they are going to hear two short biographies on history makers. They listen and take notes on their names and what they did, compare notes and listen again. Learners give their opinion of the two people, check answers and feed back to the class.

Answers

	Person	What he/she did	Why he/she is important
1	Alexander Fleming	Discovered the bacteria which was developed as penicillin	His work led to development of anti-bacterial drugs.
2	Mary Seacole	Nurse in the Crimean War	One of the first prominent black female Britons to develop nursing as a profession.

In groups of four, learners do the balloon debate. They read through the names and descriptions (or research them on the Internet). They discuss who they consider the most important individuals. Each group chooses one man and one woman in their balloon and they prepare to explain their reasoning to the class. Encourage debate and questions from the rest of the class. Alternatively, each learner can be assigned a figure who they have to represent as the most important.

Other famous people of importance

William Blake: writer, painter, visionary and human rights campaigner

Winston Churchill: leader of the UK during the Second World War

Queen Boudica: queen of the Iceni and Eastern England, fought against Roman occupation

Isambard Kingdom Brunel: designer and civil engineer

Geoffrey Chaucer: writer, poet, philosopher and diplomat

Queen Elizabeth I: voted greatest monarch of all time, in 2002 poll

Admiral Lord Nelson: celebrated military leader

Florence Nightingale: nurse and healthcare campaigner

Alan Turing: codebreaking mathematician and "father of computer science"

James Watt: inventor of steam power

Others: David Attenborough, John Logie Baird, Tim Berners-Lee, Harvey William Caxton, Edward Elgar, JK Rowling, William Tyndale

Extension

Learners can research the background of a different person from the suggestions above. Alternatively, learners could research a historic period of time, e.g. the Industrial Revolution; the reign of Henry VIII/Elizabeth I/Charles II/Queen Victoria; World War 1 or 2; the Highland Clearances; the potato famine in Ireland; the Glorious Revolution; the Norman Conquest; the English Civil War; the slave trade.

Who would you consider a 'history maker'? Listen to two people saying who they think is the most important British person in history. Take notes on each: who is the person, what did they do and why does the speaker consider them to be important?

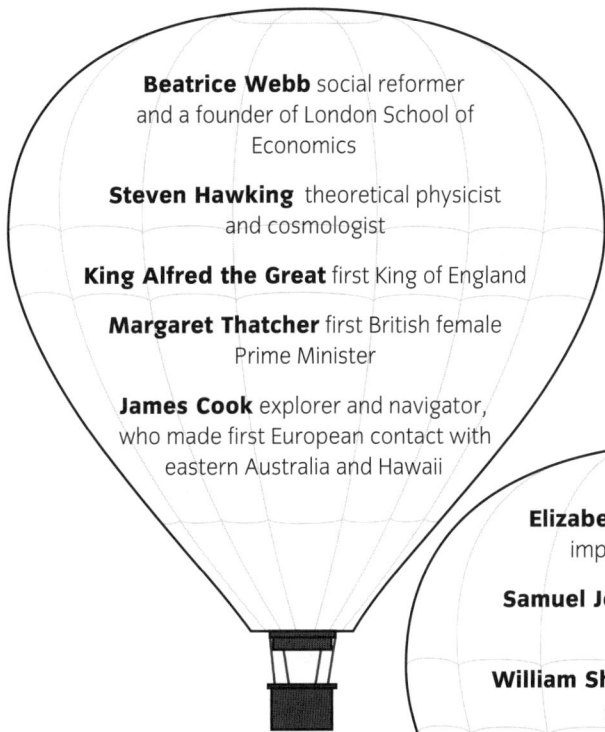

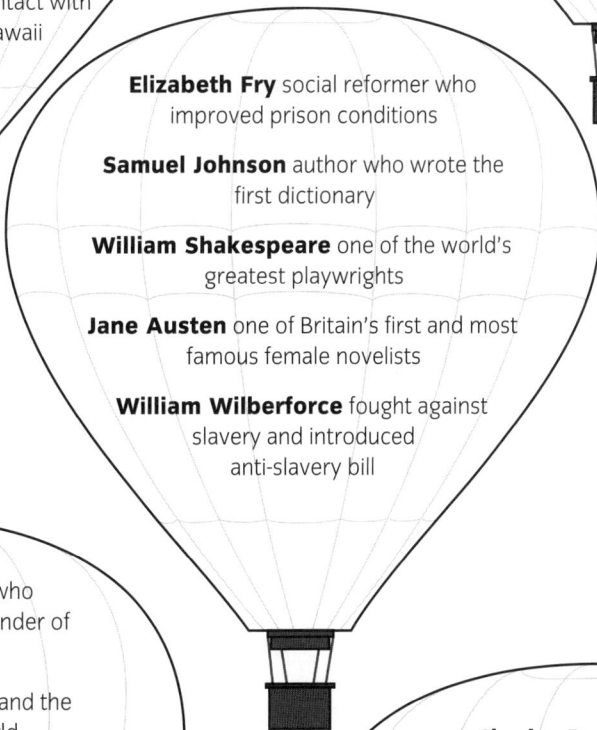

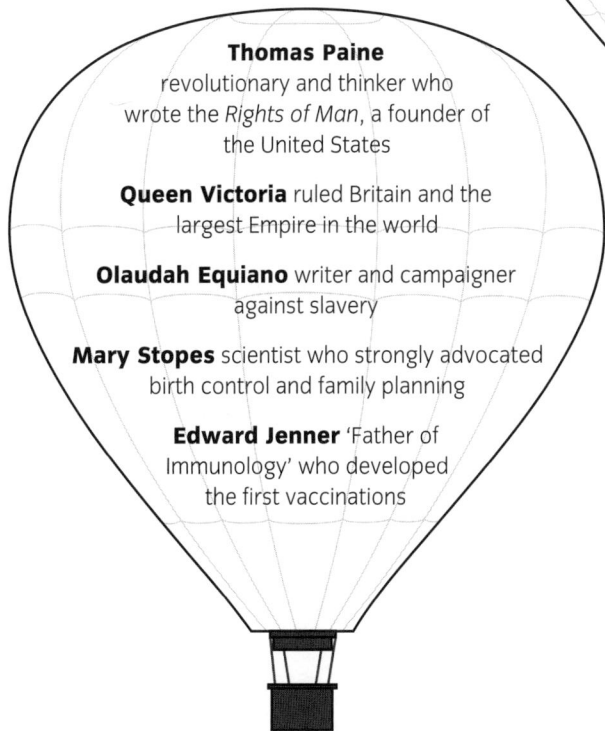

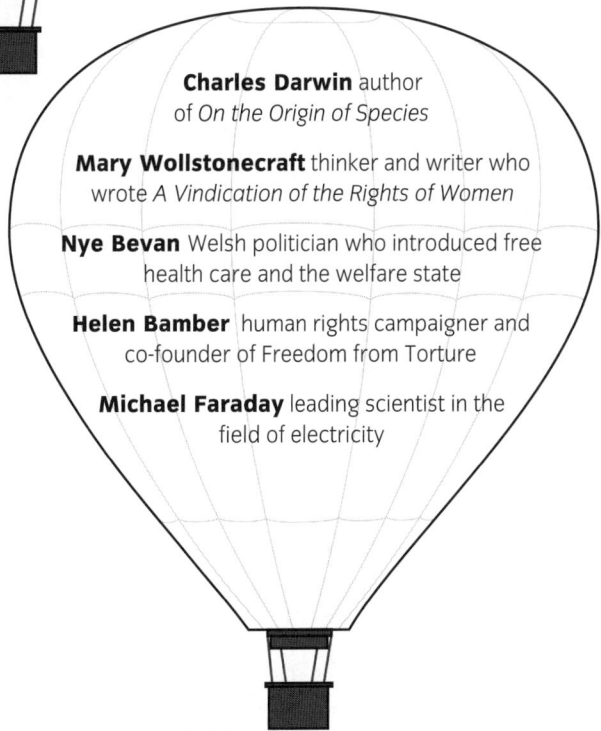

Henry VIII changed England from a Catholic to a Protestant country and unified England, Wales and Ireland

Emmeline Pankhurst campaigned for votes for women in Britain

Isaac Newton physicist and mathematician who discovered gravity and wrote the laws of motion

Diana, Princess of Wales campaigned against land mines and supported AIDS victims

John Lennon celebrated songwriter and peace campaigner

Beatrice Webb social reformer and a founder of London School of Economics

Steven Hawking theoretical physicist and cosmologist

King Alfred the Great first King of England

Margaret Thatcher first British female Prime Minister

James Cook explorer and navigator, who made first European contact with eastern Australia and Hawaii

Elizabeth Fry social reformer who improved prison conditions

Samuel Johnson author who wrote the first dictionary

William Shakespeare one of the world's greatest playwrights

Jane Austen one of Britain's first and most famous female novelists

William Wilberforce fought against slavery and introduced anti-slavery bill

Thomas Paine revolutionary and thinker who wrote the *Rights of Man*, a founder of the United States

Queen Victoria ruled Britain and the largest Empire in the world

Olaudah Equiano writer and campaigner against slavery

Mary Stopes scientist who strongly advocated birth control and family planning

Edward Jenner 'Father of Immunology' who developed the first vaccinations

Charles Darwin author of *On the Origin of Species*

Mary Wollstonecraft thinker and writer who wrote *A Vindication of the Rights of Women*

Nye Bevan Welsh politician who introduced free health care and the welfare state

Helen Bamber human rights campaigner and co-founder of Freedom from Torture

Michael Faraday leading scientist in the field of electricity

10.1

The National Health Service

TYPE OF ACTIVITY
Reading and information search

LEVEL
Elementary to Pre-intermediate

TIME
45–50 minutes

AIMS
To find out about healthcare in the UK

VOCABULARY
ambulance, book, chemist, consultant, (duty) nurse, healthcare, health insurance, insurance, on benefit, operator, out-of-hours, private, public, register, retired, surgery, system, tax, unemployed, NHS (National Health Service)

PREPARATION
One photocopy of the worksheet for each learner. Elementary dictionaries.

Warmer

Tell learners they are going to look at the British medical system. Ask them what words they can think of on the topic of health (prompt with the names of medical staff, workplaces and some illnesses). Write their responses on the board. Ask what they know about the health service in the UK. Tell them there is a national health service in Britain, i.e. a system that all people pay for in their tax. People don't pay at the time they are ill. Ask what the problems are of using a health service if travelling abroad.

1 Give a copy of the worksheet to each learner, and make dictionaries available. Focus learners on exercise 1. Learners match the words and abbreviations on the left with the meanings and check answers in pairs. Go over the answers with the class.

2 Tell learners they are going to read about the health service. Learners read the information in *The medical system*. Focus learners on exercise 2, a true/false exercise. They work in pairs to complete the exercise. Go over the answers with the class and discuss any points arising.

3 Focus learners on the *How to get medical help* leaflet. Learners read the leaflet and answer the questions. Alternatively, cut up the instructions prior to the lesson and, in pairs, learners put them in the correct order.

Answers
1 1 h 2 d 3 j 4 b 5 i 6 f 7 c 8 e 9 g 10 a
2 1 False 2 True 3 True 4 False
3 1 call 999 and ask the operator for an ambulance to hospital
   2 register with a local doctor
   3 phone the out-of-hours service and talk to them about your problem
   4 ring the surgery or book online for an appointment

4 Focus on the discussion questions. Ask them what expressions we use to talk and ask about people's opinions, e.g. *What do you think? What's your opinion on this? I think/feel that ...* Learners discuss their opinions in groups and then feed back to the class.

Extension

Learners write a short paragraph about how the healthcare system works in their country and/or compare it to the UK. Alternatively, learners could work in pairs and write dialogues around health contexts from the worksheet. Write some situational or role play cards for pairs or small groups of learners to work from, e.g. going into the doctor's surgery to register; filling in a form with a receptionist; phoning, or going in to, the surgery for an appointment; phoning for an ambulance; trying to explain about a health problem.

1 Match the words below with the meanings on the right.

1	NHS	a)	a place in hospital where patients stay during treatment
2	Dr.	b)	this takes people to hospital
3	Tel: 999	c)	take this note to a chemist (pharmacy) to get medicine
4	an ambulance	d)	short for 'doctor' (in hospitals and surgeries)
5	GP	e)	a doctor trained in a particular area of medicine
6	RN	f)	a registered nurse
7	a prescription	g)	the accident and emergency centre in a hospital
8	a consultant	h)	National Health Service
9	A&E	i)	a general practitioner is a doctor in a surgery
10	a ward	j)	ring this number in an emergency

2 Are these sentences true or false?

1 You have to pay for NHS operations in the UK. T/F

2 The NHS is paid for by tax. T/F

3 Some charity groups give you medical help. T/F

4 The NHS is the only organisation that offers counselling services. T/F

3 Read the leaflet below and answer the questions below.

1 What must you do if you need to go to hospital in an emergency?

2 What must you do before going to see a doctor?

3 What should you do if the surgery is shut?

4 How do you book an appointment to see your doctor?

The medical system

In the UK there is a National Health Service. It started in 1948 and over one million people now work in the NHS. Most people who live here can use the NHS and it is paid for by tax. Some people also pay to see private doctors and have operations using private health insurance.

Everyone in Britain must register with a GP in a doctor's surgery where they can go to the doctor about their health problems. The doctor may give you a prescription to take to a chemist or, if the problem is more serious, book an appointment with a consultant at a hospital. Most people pay a small amount of money for their medicine in the UK, unless they are unemployed, on benefit or retired. Operations are free.

The NHS also offers mental health and counselling services and services such as physiotherapy for people recovering from sporting accidents, for example, and speech therapy for people who are learning to talk again after a stroke. There are charities and other organisations that offer similar services and your doctor can tell you how to get extra help.

How to get medical help! NHS

A short guide to using the healthcare system in the UK

- Firstly you must register with a local doctor
- You should ring the surgery or book online for an appointment
- If your surgery is shut and the problem is not so serious you should phone the out-of-hours service and talk to them about your problem.
- If you have a real emergency you must call 999 and ask the operator for an ambulance to hospital.
- Give your name and address clearly to the duty nurse who will talk to you about your problem.

4 Discuss the following questions in your groups.

- What do you think about the National Health Service?
- What things are good about the British system?
- What things do you think are not so good?
- How does healthcare work in your country?
- What's similar to the system in your country?
- What's different to your country's system?

10.2

TYPE OF ACTIVITY
Matching activity and discussion

LEVEL
Intermediate

TIME
45–60 minutes

AIMS
To find out about the work of British charities

VOCABULARY
charity, cruelty, disadvantaged, environment, inspire, (be) set up, poverty, put on, raise, supporter, tackle, vulnerable

PREPARATION
One set of question and answer cards for groups of 3–4 learners. Flip chart paper and pens.

British charities

Warmer

Ask learners if they know the names of any UK charities and what they do. Alternatively, write up the short forms or acronyms of some charities and ask learners if they know what they stand for, e.g. OXFAM (Oxford Committee for Famine relief), RSPCA (Royal Society for the Prevention of Cruelty to Animals), AI (Amnesty International), NSPCC (National Society for the Prevention of Cruelty to Children).

Tell learners they're going to look at some information about important British charities. Give out one set of cards to groups of 3–4 learners and the question cards. Learners skim-read the cards and match the questions and texts. With weaker learners, check that the matches are correct. Learners then answer the questions. Go over the answers with the class. Discuss any points arising, finding out learners' views on charities: *What charities do you/would you support? Why? Which would you not support? Why? Which types of charities are the most important?*

> **Answers**
> 1 disadvantaged young people/a fundraising event when the BBC broadcasts an evening of entertainment
> 2 it works to prevent, diagnose and treat cancer and raise awareness, the British Heart Foundation raises awareness of heart disease and researches its causes and cures for it.
> 3 offers medical and psychological assistance to victims of torture and their families/write letters to support prisoners of conscience and prevent human rights abuses
> 4 disabled people/it works for higher standards in mental health care and challenges discrimination
> 5 it provides emergency shelter and support for rough sleepers/Shelter
> 6 RSPB supports the conservation of birds, RSPCA prevents cruelty and suffering of animals/WWF
> 7 works for the blind/Age UK; Save the Children Fund, Barnardo's NSPCC
> 8 by promoting and inspiring solutions to environmental problems/RNLI

Learners work in small groups. Tell them that they are secret millionaires and have decided to give some money away to charities. They have £30,000 to give to three different charities. In their groups learners discuss the charities and choose how to divide the donation. (They could briefly research the charities' websites if time allows.) When they have decided how to distribute their money they explain their decisions to the rest of the class. Option: tell them that they now have an extra £50,000 to give as a class to just one charity. Learners decide together which this will be.

For a more in-depth discussion, dictate the questions below for learners to discuss in groups. Then go over their opinions as a class.

Discussion on volunteering

What is the value of charities to society? How do charities support individuals? What kinds of activities do volunteers do in Britain? What are the benefits to people in becoming volunteers? Should governments pay for all community and social services or none at all? What charities exist in your country? What are the most/least popular? Why is this? In future, how should countries support the needs of people in their societies?

Note that most charities in the UK rely on volunteers for awareness and fundraising. Larger charities have high street shops run mostly by volunteers. Others rely on local group activities, large fundraising events and individual and business donations.

Extension

Learners research the charities' websites and explain which they find interesting. For further information on social services and healthcare in general, see *ESOL Activities Entry 2 and 3* and the website www.direct.gov.uk.

1 Who does Children in need help?

What's Red Nose Day?

Comic Relief tackles poverty in the UK and Africa. It organises Red Nose Day, a fundraising event, when the BBC broadcasts an evening of entertainment to support their work. The BBC also put on Children in Need which raises millions of pounds for disadvantaged young people.

---

2 Why is cancer research important?

How does the Heart Foundation help people?

Cancer Research UK is the biggest independent cancer research charity in the world. It works in prevention, diagnosis and treatment to reduce cancer deaths; the British Heart Foundation offers practical help, campaigns, raises awareness and researches into heart disease.

---

3 How does Freedom from Torture help people?

What do AI members do?

Amnesty International (AI) campaigns for human rights to be respected and protected. Members write letters to support prisoners of conscience and prevent human rights abuses; Freedom from Torture offers medical and psychological assistance to victims and their families.

---

4 Which group does Scope support?

Describe the work that MIND does.

MENCAP supports people with learning disabilities and their families/carers to lead full, valuable lives; MIND works for higher standards in mental health care and challenges discrimination; Scope supports disabled people to give them the same opportunities as everyone else.

---

5 What does London's big homeless charity do?

Which organisation helps with poor housing?

Shelter aims to end homelessness and bad housing. It gives advice, information and support to improve clients' lives; St Mungo's is the biggest charity for the homeless in London. It provides emergency shelter, support towards recovery and the prevention of rough sleeping.

---

6 What is the difference between the RSPB and RSPCA?

Which charity protects wild animals?

RSPCA works to prevent cruelty and suffering to animals and to raise awareness of their plight; the RSPB promotes conservation and the protection of birds and their environments; the WWF protects animals in danger of extinction throughout the world.

---

7 What does the RNIB do?

Which organisation helps the elderly/children?

Age UK aims to free disadvantaged older people from poverty, isolation and neglect; RNIB supports blind people and RNID supports the deaf; Save the Children Fund fights for children's lives and human rights; Barnardo's and NSPCC work to support all vulnerable children.

---

8 How are environmental problems reduced?

Which charity rescues people from the sea?

RNLI (Royal Navy Lifeboat Institute) funds sea rescue by volunteers; Oxfam is a global movement of people working to overcome poverty and suffering; Friends of the Earth makes life better for people by promoting and inspiring solutions to environmental problems.

The welfare state

TYPE OF ACTIVITY
Reading gap fill, listening and discussion

LEVEL
Advanced

TIME
45–60 minutes

AIMS
To gain an understanding of the British welfare state

VOCABULARY
ancillary, civil servant, cut back, income support, local government, maternity benefits, medical practitioner, public sector, superannuation scheme, tax threshold, welfare state

PREPARATION
One photocopy of the worksheet and audio script for each learner. Dictionary for each pair of learners or group.

Warmer

Tell learners they're going to find out about the welfare state. Write up the title – in pairs/ groups learners define it: a system whereby the government provides free social services, for health, education and sickness and unemployment support. Go over their responses and elicit other vocabulary related to the topic, e.g. *the public sector, social services, the benefit system, an allowance*; and types of jobs associated with the public sector and local government, e.g. *medical staff / healthcare workers, ancillary staff (cleaners, porters, etc.), police, firemen, teachers, care assistants, local council officers, bus drivers, refuse collectors, gardeners, housing/welfare officers, traffic wardens, civil servants* – but not the military.

Give a copy of the worksheet to each learner. Learners read the report introduction. Ask them what five issues the report will cover; analyse concerns about the system, outline the history, identify key developments, discuss the benefits and constraints, offer findings.

1 Learners read about the formation of the welfare system and complete the gap fill activity. They check in pairs, using dictionaries as required, then answer the questions. Go over the answers with the class.

> **Answers**
> **1 1** developments **2** stages **3** society **4** infirm **5** basic **6** Pensions **7** reform **8** institutions
> **2 1** as a response to poverty in northern cities and as a reflection of a change of attitudes and expectations of British people after WWII
> **2** simple pension, sickness insurance and a basic unemployment benefit scheme
> **3** in 1948 by a radical Labour government
> **4** it is free to people at the point of delivery

Welfare State Debate

▶ 41 Tell learners that they are going to listen to three people discussing issues around the British welfare system. Focus learners on the pre-listening task, anticipating the arguments for and against a state welfare system. Learners listen and take notes. Go over their responses as a class. Option: learners read the script and discuss the arguments made in more detail. Go over the arguments with the class, explaining any terminology where necessary.

> **Answers**
> **1 Speaker A:** NHS supports a lot of people's needs; supports sick, disabled and unemployed; better system than the past; fairer society; paid for by tax
> **Speaker B:** all dental and eye treatment are not included; have to wait longer for treatment; unsustainable; ageing population; nothing left to support our children
> **Speaker C:** too expensive; the rich have to pay for the poor; encourages people to be lazy
> **2** It is important to everyone in the UK as nearly everyone uses it. However, there are concerns about the cost and quality of care and these concerns are constantly being debated.

Learners discuss and evaluate the benefits and constraints of the system. Encourage them to further consider the advantages and disadvantages to the system. Conclude the discussion by inviting learners to compare the system with their own country.

Extension

There is an opportunity for learners to develop their writing skills by completing the report. Working in pairs, learners can research the next sections and produce a collaborative report. These can then be compared in class and their findings analysed. Alternatively, learners can take part in a class debate, discussing the advantages and disadvantages of a public welfare system.

Below is a part of a recent report on the British welfare system. Read the introduction and identify how the report will be structured. Then answer the questions below.

The British welfare system
Report

This report aims to analyse concerns about the future of the British welfare system. It will offer a brief outline of the history of welfare services in Britain and the National Health Service (NHS), and identify key [1] _____ within the service. It will then discuss the benefits and constraints of the publicly funded British welfare services in contrast to privately run services. The report's findings will be offered as a conclusion.

The formation of the welfare system

The British welfare state was set up in [2] _____ from the beginning of the 20th century. It was established for the great part as a response to the terrible poverty in northern British cities as a result of the Industrial Revolution. The movement of people from countryside to city to take up work changed the structure of [3] _____ and local communities could no longer be relied on to support welfare of the sick, the elderly and the [4] _____ . Some support was offered to the poor in the form of a simple pension, sickness insurance and a [5] _____ unemployment benefit scheme, introduced by the Liberal government from 1906–14 in a series of Acts of Parliament, including the Old Age [6] _____ Act of 1908 and the National Insurance Act of 1911. The 'People's Budget' of 1909 reformed the tax system in order to fund this revolutionary social [7] _____ . After World War II, a Labour government was elected with a mandate for social reform, which reflected a great change in people's attitudes and expectations. In 1948 the government passed the National Health Act, bringing in sweeping changes to healthcare, introducing compulsory national insurance payments and setting up the NHS, which is free to people at the point of delivery and one of the most popular and fiercely supported public [8] _____ in the country.

1 **Put the words below into the correct gaps in the article.**

basic   developments   infirm   institutions   society   stages   reform   Pensions

2 **Answer the questions below.**

1   What were the reasons for the establishment of the welfare state?

2   What support was offered to poor people prior to World War II?

3   When was it set up and by whom?

4   Why is the NHS so popular?

The Welfare State Debate

1   Listen to the debate. What opinions does each person express and what reasons do they give for them?

2   Why do you think the speakers are so passionate about the welfare system?

Discuss the following questions in your groups.

• Which of the three speakers do you agree with and why?

• How does the welfare and health system in Britain differ from that in your country?

• What do you think are the benefits of the NHS in comparison to a privately funded system? What are the disadvantages?

• How do other aspects of the British Welfare System compare in general to those of your country? How do they differ from your system?

How the British relax

TYPE OF ACTIVITY
Listening for information and discussion

LEVEL
Elementary to Pre-intermediate

TIME
40–50 minutes

AIMS
To find out what British people do in their free time

VOCABULARY
armchair sportsman, concert, cool, gardening, have a laugh, interest, leisure, mate, referee, weed

PREPARATION
One photocopy of the worksheet for each learner.

Warmer

Write *interests and hobbies* on the board. Check that learners understand the meanings. Elicit any hobbies that learners can think of and write these on the board. From the list, ask learners which interests they think are popular in the UK. Tick each activity from the list on the board (football, shopping, going to the pub, etc.)

1 Tell learners that they're going to find out what some British people enjoy doing in their free time. Give a worksheet to each learner. Focus on the pairs of pictures. They match the words to the pictures and write the answers above the pictures. Go over the answers with the class.

2 ▶ 42–46 Tell learners that they're going to hear some people talking about an activity they enjoy. They listen to the five conversations and tick the activity spoken about. They listen then check in pairs.

3 Play the audio again for learners to answer the questions in exercise 3 and again check in pairs. Go over their answers with the class.

4 Focus on exercise 4, the vocabulary matching activity. Learners complete the activity in pairs. Go over their answers with the class. Ask learners which list is more informal language and which is more formal (1–5 informal, a–e formal).

> ### Answers
> 1 a pub b restaurant c theatre d cinema e football stadium f TV
>   g walking h gardening i concert j club
> 2 1 the pub (a) 2 the theatre (c) 3 TV (f) 4 gardening (h) 5 a concert (i)
> 3 1 her friends (mates)
>   2 because it's different, interesting
>   3 football
>   4 the hard work
>   5 you can go any time; it's not that exciting
> 4 1 d 2 e 3 a 4 c 5 b

5 Focus on the discussion. Prepare the questions learners need to ask with the class using the question prompts. Learners work in pairs or groups of three to find out what interests their partners have. Learners write down the answers under their partners' names. They then go round the class, finding out and writing down other learners' interests. Find out the most popular interests, as a class survey, counting votes for top activities

Extension

Display more photos of some unusual activities that people do in the UK (these can be obtained from the Internet). These could include: Morris Men, Medieval fairs and banquets, archery, the Highland Games, Red Nose Day events, fun runs, Irish dancing, collectors of strange objects, DIY (working on houses is extremely popular in the UK).

1   Match the words below with the pictures.

cinema   concert   club

pub   restaurant   football stadium

gardening   theatre   TV

walking

A ....   B ....

C ....   D ....   E ....   F ....

G ....   H ....   I ....   J ....

2   Listen to people talking about what they like doing in their free time. Tick the correct picture. Check your answers with your partner.

3   Listen to the audio again. Answer the following questions.

1   Who does the young girl go to the pub with on a Saturday night?

2   Why does the woman like going to the theatre?

3   What sport did the old man used to do?

4   What does the man do in the garden?

5   What does the woman say about going to a club?

What people say!

4   Look at the informal language below and match the words with the meanings.

1   the telly   a   yes

2   it's cool   b   to have fun

3   yeah   c   a friend

4   a mate   d   the television

5   to have a laugh   e   it's OK or good

5   In your free time …

• Work in groups. Tell your partners three things you like doing in your free time. Ask them where and how often they do these things.

• Find out from everyone in your class what they like doing. Make a list of the top 10 things that people do.

• Find out unusual interests that people have.

Some British pastimes

11.2

TYPE OF ACTIVITY
Reading and information exchange

LEVEL
Intermediate

TIME
45–60 minutes

AIMS
To find out more about how British people socialise

VOCABULARY
amateur, bar, cider, counter, depict, good loser, gymkhana, horse riding, horse shoe, karaoke, league, marathon, myth, participant, pint, professional, socialise, spectator, stand for

PREPARATION
One photocopy of the worksheet for each pair of learners, cut into Cards A and B. Option: display pictures of British pubs and sporting events.

Warmer

Tell learners they are going to look at two typical ways British people spend their free time. Write the words *sport* and *pubs* on the board. Ask learners if they know the names of any famous sporting events in the UK and what they know about pubs. Elicit any related vocabulary, e.g. popular drinks, names/types of pubs, opening times, typical pub food. Write their answers on the board. Discuss their comments with the class.

Examples
FA and Scottish FA Cup Finals (national football tournament watched by millions); Wimbledon, international tennis; international golf at St Andrews in Scotland; Six Nations (rugby); the London Marathon; the Ashes (cricket); Royal Ascot, the Grand National and the Derby (horse racing); the 2012 Olympics; Silverstone Grand Prix (motor racing).

Option 1: pair work
Learners work in pairs. Give out Card A to one learner in a pair and Card B to the other. They read through the information card, checking the meanings of any new words. Then learners ask their partner the significance of the letters at the bottom of each card. Give an example, e.g. *What does the letter P stand for?* Learners exchange information and, when they've finished, swap cards and read their partner's card. Go over answers with the class.

Option 2: wall dictation
Place enlarged photocopies of the two texts on the walls in the room. Learners work in groups of four. Copy the initial letters onto cards and place them in piles on the tables. They go up to the wall one by one, find the information matching the letter and tell the rest of their group the information. Learners write down the key points. Go over the answers with the class.

Learners do the discussion questions in groups. Give out one card to each pair/group. Go over the answers with the class.

> **Answers**
> 2   cricket
> 3   hold quiz nights and sports events, darts, pool and skittles and have 'Karaoke' nights; Desi pubs have singing and dancing
> 4   Great North Run, London Marathon
> 5   some sports events happen in pubs/people relax after watching sport/people watch sports on TV
> 6   they order from the bar

Extension

Learners research some sporting activities and national or local events. Smaller but interesting events include the Scottish Highland Games, various places in Scotland; the World Bog Snorkelling Championships, Llanwrtyd Wells, Wales; Robert Dover's Games, Cotswolds, England; Man Versus Horse Marathon, Wales; The World Toe Wrestling Competition (first started in a pub in Derbyshire, England); Cheese rolling, Gloucester, England. Learners report back on these to the class and add them to their British culture book/blog.

A

Pubs A very important part of British life is the pub. Here, people of all ages and occupations socialise, but not always together. Over three quarters of adults go to pubs and over a third of them are regulars, going to the same one at least twice a week.

Halves and pints People still buy lager, cider and real ale (traditional British beer) in pints and half-pints. This system was used before Britain became metric – a pint is 568ml.

Desi pubs are pubs run by British Asians where music, singing and dancing are popular. Nowadays, other people go to these pubs too after work or even after a football game.

Bar The rooms in pubs were once called 'saloon' or 'lounge' bars, which were more comfortable and more expensive, and 'public' bars – the names still exist but today there is little difference. At the bar, strangers often start a conversation together. Customers buy their drinks and order food here and it's one of the few places where you don't have to queue – but people will frown at you, if you push in.

Names Pub names and signs often tell us about famous people and events. The signs are often very attractively painted. Pub signs were very important in the days when many people couldn't read.

Country pubs Some people drive to a country pub in the evenings or at weekends for a drink or to have a nice meal. Traditional country pubs are old, with wooden beamed ceilings, log fires, with horse brasses, old pictures decorating the walls and beer gardens.

Entertainment can be really varied. Lots of pubs hold quiz nights and sports events. Many also provide darts, pool and even skittles for the locals. Some pubs even have 'Karaoke' nights. Originally from Japan, this has become very popular in Britain. Often people watch sports events on pub TVs.

Rounds If you go to the pub with a group of people, you may have to buy a 'round' of drinks. Each person takes a turn to buy everyone else a drink – this can be very expensive!

Ask your partner what these letters stand for: S J C U H R G F

B

Sport is a popular form of entertainment in Britain, enjoyed by professionals and amateurs, adults and children. Traditionally, British people like a good loser, an underdog or a good amateur who tries hard.

Cricket is less popular than football, but it's the typical British summer sport, played by town and village teams – the idea of 'fair play' is very important. Some international matches last for five days!

Greyhound racing is less popular than it used to be though there are still stadiums in many towns and cities. Pigeon racing is also still practised and some people keep them in their back gardens. Bird watching is also popular.

Football is the most popular sport in Britain and millions of people follow league games in winter. There are many local men's teams but women's football is quite strong too. England came second in the Women's European Cup in 2009, beaten in the final by Germany.

Horses Horse racing is popular and people gamble on horses to get a 'winner'. The Royal Family own race horses and attend the Ascot race meeting every summer. Riding is also popular – people go to local stables and some in the summer enter competitions, called 'gymkhanas' and 'point to points'.

Jogging In the UK, it's very common to see people running to keep fit, whatever the weather. There are also big races like the Great North Run and the London Marathon. Thousands of amateurs run to support their charities.

Rugby There are two types of this tough winter sport. Traditionally working-class Rugby League is most popular in the north of England while Rugby Union, sometimes seen as more middle class, is more popular in the rest of the UK.

Unusual sports As well as normal things like boxing, motor sports, cycling, sailing and swimming, there are a number of more eccentric events like cheese rolling and ditch snorkelling.

Ask your partner what these letters stand for: P B E C H D N R

Put your cards together.

1 Underline any new words and discuss their meanings.
2 What's the most popular summer sport in the UK?
3 What entertainments do people do in pubs?
4 Can you name two British marathons?
5 What connections are there between pubs and sport in Britain?
6 How do people buy food and drink in pubs?
7 How do people like to pass their time in your country?

Taking time out

TYPE OF ACTIVITY
Listening for information and discussion

LEVEL
Advanced

TIME
50–60 minutes

AIMS
To gain awareness of social events in the UK

VOCABULARY
cower, day trip, get soaked/sodden, iconic, media, medieval fair, pageant, ramble, stare, straddle, wildlife park, while away time, the National Trust

PREPARATION
One photocopy of the worksheet for each learner.
Option: display pictures of famous events or places of interest around the UK.

Warmer

Tell learners they're going to look at some ways British people spend their free time. Ask them if they know any popular/famous events that take place in the UK (prompt with music, arts, sport). Write *festivals* (i.e. lasting for a few days/weeks), *national events* (a day or weekend) and *places of interest* (for a day out) on the board. Ask learners what categories their suggestions would go under. Learners categorise the activities in pairs/groups. Useful prompts could be pictures of events given out as a quiz for learners to match with their titles, written on the board.

Examples
Festivals: Celtic Connections, Edinburgh Festival (Scotland); Eisteddfod, Hay-on-Wye book festival (Wales); Belfast Titanic/Arts Festival (Northern Ireland); Notting Hill Carnival, Glastonbury (England)
Events: the (University) Boat Race, the Lord Mayor's Show, Last Night of the Proms
Places of interest: Hampton Court Palace, Edinburgh Castle, Windsor Castle, York Minster, Brighton Pavilion, Caernarfon Castle.

Part A ▶ 47–51 Give a copy of the worksheet to each learner. Focus on the images and ask if they recognise any of the events. Read the introduction and tell learners they're going to hear five people talking about events they've been to. Play the audio while learners match the events with the images. Learners check their answers in pairs.

Play the audio again for them to write notes about each festival. Go over the answers with the class.

Answers
1 **a** Titanic **b** Brighton Festival **c** Highland Games **d** Hay-on-Wye **e** WOMAD
2 **a** Titanic Festival: boating and arts festival/all the family/most people have a fabulous week/better if you like boats
   b Brighton Festival: arts festival/all ages and backgrounds/see great performances in a very relaxed city right by the sea; tickets are expensive and sell out early
   c Highland Games: sports festivals/everyone would enjoy these quirky and unique/the midges are a problem
   d Hay-on-Wye: literary, debate and performing arts/brings people who love performing together; book your accommodation (B&B) early
   e WOMAD Festival: world music/college students/the music and atmosphere are cool and atmosphere fun/it can rain really hard

Part B Focus learners on Part B, *Britain's Heritage*. Learners read the texts and answer the questions, checking their answers in pairs.

Answers
1 (bridleway) a pathway for people and horses; (ramble) to wander/walk mostly used for the countryside; (stately home) a large country house; (straddle) to stretch between
2 The writer is concerned that the British may not value the amazing amount of heritage that they have.

Learners do the discussion activity in groups. Go over their responses. Ask learners to compare commercialisation and tourist development within Britain and with their own countries.

Extension

Learners prepare a travel article on two or three of the places to deliver to the class or plan an itinerary of a route round Britain, taking in some iconic sites and places of interest (suggestions: the New Forest, St Davids, Windsor Castle, Antrim plateau, Bath, Canterbury, Durham, the Lake District, Holy Island, Hadrian's Wall).

A

Out and about in the UK

Britain has fewer national holidays than most other countries in Europe and it doesn't really have any breaks specific to a region or locality. As a consequence, people make a great effort to get out at the weekend, taking day trips to the country or the seaside.

a ....

1 You are going to hear several people talking about festivals and events that take place annually in the UK.

b ....

c ....

1 Identify the events and match them to the photos on the right. Write in the names of the events.

2 Listen again and find out …

- what kind of festivals and events these are

- the people who would enjoy these events

- the positive aspects of the events

- something you are warned about

Read what the American author Bill Bryson writes about British

d ....

e ....

B

Britain's heritage

Britain's cultural heritage is extensive and there are countless ways people while away the time taking in the sights. They visit private stately homes, open houses, National Trust properties, gardens and parkland, or ramble on footpaths and bridleways that straddle the countryside.

heritage.

1 Answer the following questions.

> It sometimes occurs to me that the British have more heritage than is good for them. Consider the numbers: 445,000 listed buildings, 12,000 medieval churches, 120,000 miles of footpaths and public rights of ways … in my Yorkshire village alone there are more 17th century buildings than in the whole of North America.
>
> Extract from *Notes from a Small Island* by Bill Bryson

1 What is the meaning of the following words

bridleway   ramble   stately home   straddle

2 What does the writer feel is unappreciated?

2 Do you think that a country can have too much heritage? Why/Why not?

3 Discuss the following questions in your groups.

- Which of the events or places would you like to visit most? Why?

- What is the most interesting festival or event in your country?

- What places of interest would you recommend a tourist to visit?

- What new place or building would you protect as a World Heritage site in your country?

- What is your view on the conservation of old buildings versus the development of new ones?

- What are the benefits and constraints of the tourist industry to a country?

12.1

News in the UK

TYPE OF ACTIVITY
Reading and information search

LEVEL
Elementary to Pre-intermediate

TIME
45–60 minutes

AIMS
To find out how British people communicate

VOCABULARY
broadcast, century, ceremony, channel, communication, crown, media, mp3 player, neighbour, popular, publish, technology, BBC (British Broadcasting Corporation), ITV (Independent Television), Internet, Smartphone

PREPARATION
One photocopy of the worksheet for each learner, cut in half. Cut up the reading cards and headings.

Warmer

Ask learners for different ways that they communicate or talk together. Write their responses on the board. Tell learners that British people often communicate by text and email as well as mobile phone, and social networking is popular too. Ask them why they think this is. Then ask learners how they get information, how important they think newspapers are now, and why.

Ways to communicate: mobile phones, texts, emails, Internet, social networking (Twitter), blogs, video

Traditional ways to receive information: newspapers, radio, TV, landline phones, letters and cards

Tell learners they're going to find out about the UK media.

Option 1: information search
Learners work in pairs/threes. Give out one set of reading cards and headings to each pair. Learners read the cards and match the headings with the information. Check the answers with the class. They then put the paragraphs in the correct order (use the dates as clues). Go over the correct order with the group (see worksheet for complete text). Give out the second half of the worksheet. Focus learners on the questions (exercise 1). Learners find the answers to the questions. Go over answers with the class.

Option 2: wall dictation
Pin copies of the texts (cut up, enlarged) on the wall. Give out the second half of the worksheet. Learners work in groups of three. One finds the answer to a question (exercise 1) from the walls, returns to their group and dictates the answer. The next learner repeats this process until all the questions have been answered (this can also be done as a race). Go over answers with the class.

> **Answers**
> **1** **1** six radio stations came together and the BBC was born
> **2** in the 1980s
> **3** 20 million/1953
> **4** a national newspaper/1785
> **5** 1936/www.bbc.co.uk
> **6** About half their time

2 Focus learners on exercise 2, the gap fill activity and discussion. Go over the answers with the class.

> **Answers**
> **2** **1** newspapers
> **2, 3** television; radio
> **4–6** computers/Internet; smartphones; social networking

3 Learners do the discussion activity. This can be done with the whole class or as a small group activity, depending on their level.

Extension

Learners make a photographic display of different British newspapers (see the list in Unit 12.2 worksheet) or TV programmes (the BBC website shows the range of services offered). See BBC Skillswise for interesting English language activities. Learners can see original videos of the coronation of Queen Elizabeth II and other events on the Internet. Information found can be added to their British culture book/blog. Teachers can review the future simple form to discuss future events.

The beginning of national news

Today there are many different ways to find out about the news. In 1621 in London the first British newspaper was called the *Corante*. The national newspaper *The Times* was first published in 1785. Now there are ten national newspapers in the UK and many weekend and local papers.

The birth of radio

In the 1890s, an Italian man called Marconi worked on early radio in London. At this time in Britain the cinema was an important way to find out about news stories. In 1922 six radio stations came together and the BBC was born. Today more people than ever listen to radio.

The first televisions

In 1936, the BBC broadcast the first television programmes from London. At first people didn't think that TV would be popular. In 1953, when Queen Elizabeth II was crowned, over 20 million British people watched the ceremony on TV and millions more worldwide. Now there are a lot of independent channels and all television is digital.

The start of computers

In the UK, computers were first sold in the shops in the 1980s. After this, lots of British people bought computers. Then the Internet became a very popular way to get information and to talk together. People say they spend about half their time using technology and media.

From smartphones to social networking

Many British people like using mobile phones and other types of technology. Smartphones are very popular and people often text using a simple spelling form. Communication is very fast because of texting and social networking (like Twitter and Facebook). These are also important at work and in education.

The news today

Today, the BBC is still very important, in the UK and abroad, with more channels and different ways to find the news. www.bbc.co.uk is a popular news and information website. There are also many private companies that show news programmes and newspapers with their own websites – but you have to pay for some.

1 **Answer the questions from the text.**

1 What happened in 1922?

2 When were the first computers sold in shops in the UK?

3 How many people watched Queen Elizabeth's coronation on TV and when was this?

4 What is *The Times* and when was it published?

5 When did BBC TV start? What is the BBC website address?

6 How much of their time do British people use technology?

2 **Fill in the gaps in the sentences below.**

3 **Discuss the following questions in your groups.**

- What technology do you have? What would you like to have?

- How do you like to get news and information?

- How are people going to do this in the future?

- Will people still buy newspapers? What will these be like?

- Will people watch TV or listen to the radio? If not, what will they do?

- What changes are good and what are bad? Why?

Communication in the UK

In Britain, ¹ .... first gave people information in the 17th century.

In the middle of the 20th century ² .... and ³ .... became important.

Now people also use ⁴ .... , ⁵ .... and ⁶ .... to get information.

12.2

In the news

TYPE OF ACTIVITY
Reading, listening and discussion

LEVEL
Intermediate

TIME
50–60 minutes

AIMS
To find out information about British newspapers

VOCABULARY
article, broadsheet, circulation, column, gossip, headline, in-depth, left-wing, on sale, quality, right-wing, sales, tabloid

PREPARATION
One photocopy of the worksheet per learner. Display some copies or pictures of British newspapers.

Warmer

Ask learners the names of any national British newspapers and write them on the board. Then ask what they know about them. Show them some examples/pictures of British newspapers and discuss them. Prompt with *Which is a tabloid/a broadsheet? Which are more serious newspapers?* Discuss which papers contain more human interest stories and gossip (*tabloid*) and which have more political and world news (*broadsheet*). Ask if newspapers in Britain are privately-owned or government-owned (*they are privately owned*).

1 Tell learners they're going to find out more about British newspapers. Give a copy of the worksheet to each learner. Focus on the article. Learners read the information, answer the questions and check in pairs. Go over the answers with the class. Invite learners to compare the types of newspapers and magazines with their own countries.

2 ▶ 52–56 Tell learners they are going to hear five short dialogues. Ask them to listen and match the person to the newspaper they read. Go over the answers with the class. Then, in pairs, they discuss personal information about each person, e.g. age, job or past job, family (married/single, children), social class, financial status, politics.

Answers

1 1 F (just over 2 m)   5 T
   2 T   6 T
   3 F (the right)   7 T
   4 F (10)   8 F (it's a magazine)
2 1 The Guardian
   2 The Times, Financial Times and The Telegraph
   3 The Sun
   4 Daily Mail or Daily Express
   5 The Independent

3 Learners then do the second part of the listening activity, exercise 3. Working in pairs, ask learners to write down why people read a particular paper. Go over the answers with the class and discuss any points arising.

Answers

3 1 The Guardian has articles about education and job advertisements, and covers world news thoroughly.
   2 The woman prefers The Times to any other paper; the man likes the Financial Times for financial news and The Telegraph for sports.
   3 The Sun has a lot of sports reports and is smaller and cheaper than other papers.
   4 The Daily Mail and Daily Express are good family newspapers.
   5 The woman doesn't like newspapers; the man likes The Independent to find out what's happening in the world.

4 Focus learners on the discussion questions. Learners work in groups of 3–4. Go over their responses and any further points with the class. You can also explain that children from 13 can deliver papers before going to school and at weekends but the hours and times are limited. Find out if this is similar in their countries.

Extension

Choose three or four articles from a newspaper and make four or five reading and vocabulary activities from these. Pin the activities up round the room. Also write an answer and score sheet. Learners move round the room completing the tasks, scoring points for correct answers. This can be done as a timed activity. Example activities: find four or five articles and a cartoon. Enlarge them to A3 size. Take the headlines from four articles. Learners match the story to the headline (4 points). Take an article, blank out four key words and write them underneath. Learners complete the gap fill (4 points). Cut up a cartoon for learners to sequence in the correct order (1 point for each correct place). Take a short story and cut up the paragraphs. Learners sequence them in the correct order (4 points).
Display the front of a newspaper. Ask what sections are called: a column, a headline, a leader, an article (4 points).

Newspapers in the UK

In the UK there are 10 major national daily newspapers and about 60 local ones. Britain has no government-owned papers but national newspapers often reflect the politics of their owners.

Many people buy daily newspapers, although sales have fallen in recent years. Weekend papers are popular for their information on sport, media and food, and their travel and fashion supplements.

Large newspapers which contain more national and international news are called broadsheets.

Papers with lots of photos and sport are called tabloids. They are usually smaller in size and full of celebrity gossip and stories. There are popular magazines like *Take a Break* and *Heat* and hundreds of specialist journals on sale too.

The paper with the highest circulation with nearly 3 million copies sold a day is *The Sun*. It's also the cheapest to buy. Next comes the *Daily Mail* (just over 2 million) followed by the *Daily Mirror* (1.2 million). Scotland has its own national papers but the UK broadsheets are popular there too.

The newspapers to the left of politics are the *Daily Mirror* and *The Guardian*. *The Independent* holds the centre ground with no linked political views. Newspapers such as the *Daily Mail*, *The Times* and *The Telegraph* are to the right.

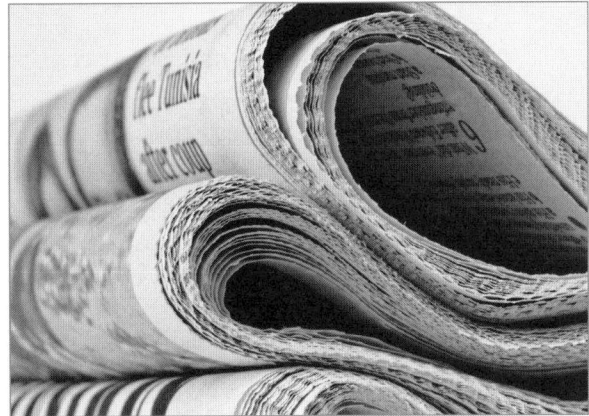

1 Are the following statements true or false?

1	The *Daily Mail* has a circulation of 3 million.	T/F
2	Tabloid newspapers contain a lot of gossip.	T/F
3	*The Times* is to the left of politics.	T/F
4	There are 20 major newspapers in the UK.	T/F
5	There are different newspapers in Scotland.	T/F
6	Weekend papers include information on travel.	T/F
7	There is one politically independent broadsheet newspaper.	T/F
8	*Heat* is a popular newspaper.	T/F

2 Listen to the audio. Which newspaper does each person read?

1 .... 2 .... 3 .... 4 .... 5 ....

3 Listen again and write down why each person buys their newspaper.

1 ....

2 ....

3 ....

4 ....

5 ....

4 Discuss the following questions in your groups.

- What do you prefer to read, newspapers or magazines?
- What do you think is more interesting to read, local or world news? Why?
- How important are newspapers now to get information?
- What other ways do you get information?
- What is your opinion of British magazines and gossip papers?
- In the future, how do you think we will get our news?

12.3

TYPE OF ACTIVITY
Listening quiz and discussion

LEVEL
Advanced

TIME
45–60 minutes

AIMS
To gain an understanding of the importance of the BBC

VOCABULARY
broadcast, charter, cut, dumb down, fulfil, in accordance with, inspire, licence payer, network, nickname, rating, realm, upgrade

PREPARATION
One photocopy of worksheet and audio script for each learner.

The BBC

Warmer

Tell learners they're going to look at the role and importance of the BBC. Ask if they know of, or have any favourite British TV or radio programmes. Write their responses on the board. Ask what these programmes are about. Find out if they know of the areas in which the BBC is also important (national and local radio, the BBC World Service, production of internationally recognised documentaries and entertainment, BBC iPlayer, educational websites and forums such as Skillswise). Ask learners what makes the BBC different to commercial TV channels (*there is no commercial advertising on the BBC*).

▶ 57 Give a copy of the worksheet to each learner. Learners look at the *The BBC Quiz*. Learners work in pairs or threes and guess the answers. Play the audio for learners to check their answers. Go over the answers and ask what most surprises or interests them, e.g the licence fee, independence from the government.

> **Answers**
> **Quiz: 1** c **2** b **3** b **4** b **5** c **6** b **7** c **8** c **9** a **10** a **11** a **12** a
> **Dumbing down:** striking a balance between maintaining high-quality programmes and attracting large audiences

▶ 58 Focus learners on Part 2 of the audio, discussing the role of the BBC. Ask learners what they understand by the expression *to dumb down* (to make something more populist and of less substance). Learners listen and take brief notes. Discuss the arguments raised with the class. Learners discuss the three aims of the BBC in its charter (to educate, entertain and inform), the role of the BBC and the conflicts it faces. Learners do the final discussion activity in groups.

Invite learners to compare the equivalent media services or TV programmes with those in their countries and evaluate the advantages and disadvantages of government-run and privately-run media, with or without a licence fee, as a class/group discussion.

Extension

Learners research on the web the range of BBC sites including: BBC TV; BBC World Service; BBC World News and local stations; BBC iPlayer, www.bbc.co.uk; educational sites: CBBC, Cbeebies, BBC Skillswise. In groups, learners report back to the class as small workshop sessions, giving a presentation and tour around the site, or aspects of the site they have been looking at. Learners can also research developments in technology and report on how these may affect communication in the future.

The BBC Quiz

What do you know about the BBC?
Look at the questionnaire below and circle your answers.

1   Who is the main broadcaster in the UK?
    a Sky   b Fox   c BBC

2   When did BBC TV first start to broadcast?
    a 1926   b 1936   c 1948

3   About how many people does the BBC employ?
    a 10,000   b 20,000   c 30,000

4   What is the BBC's nickname?
    a Daddy   b Auntie   c Granny

5   Where is the main centre of the BBC?
    a Manchester   b Bristol   c London

6   What is the name of a famous BBC programme?
    a Dr No   b Dr Who   c Animal Dr

7   How many million people listen to the world service?
    a 25 m   b 95 m   c 160 m

8   How many capital cities can get BBC world service on FM?
    a 55   b 95   c 150+

9   Until 1967, the only UK radio service permitted to broadcast was the BBC.
    a True   b False

10 The BBC is independent of the British government.
    a True   b False

11 All British households must pay to receive the BBC.
    a True   b False

12 The BBC is the largest broadcaster in the world.
    a True   b False

Dumbing down

Listen to the rest of the conversation. What is the challenge that faces the BBC?

What do you think?

1   Why is it important that the BBC is free from government?

2   Why is it important that it is free from advertising?

3   Discuss the BBC's three main responsibilities and put them in order of importance:

• to educate

• to entertain

• to inform

Which of the following kinds of programmes provide the most important public service? Which do you watch most?

News and current affairs   reality TV   soap operas   quiz shows

sports broadcasts   celebrity news   documentaries

lifestyle, e.g. cookery, DIY   drama   comedy   children's TV

Discuss the following questions in groups.

• What are the advantages and disadvantages of a publicly-run TV service?

• What about privately-run services?

• In your country, what programmes are popular?

• How would you improve television services?

13.1

The learning journey

**TYPE OF
ACTIVITY**
Listening and
reading, gap fill

LEVEL
Elementary to Pre-
intermediate

TIME
45–60 minutes

AIMS
To find out about
the British education
system

VOCABULARY
adult education,
college of further
education, crèche,
degree, exam,
nursery school,
primary school
(infant school, junior
school), naughty,
school dinner,
secondary school,
sixth form college,
GCSE, A-level, BA/
BSc

PREPARATION
One photocopy of
the worksheet for
each learner.
Photocopies of the
script as required.

Warmer

Ask learners what they know about the education system in the UK. Write their responses on the board. Ask them the names of the different types of school children attend. Alternatively, write the names of the different schools on sets of cards (nursery school, primary school, secondary school, sixth form college, college of further education/university). Give out sets to groups of 3-4 learners and ask them to put them in the correct order, starting with schools for young children first.

1 ▶ 59 Give a copy of the worksheet to each learner. Focus on the true/false statements. Discuss any ideas that may not be familiar to learners, e.g. school dinners. Learners discuss and guess the answers in pairs. Play the audio for learners to check their answers. Ask them to check their work in pairs. Go over answers with the class.

2 Learners guess the ages that children start the different stages of education in England, or leave school. Learners write in their answers in the 'England' box. Tell them the answers. Then learners fill in the same information about their own country. Learners discuss the differences in pairs or as a class. Discuss any surprises that they found. Discuss or note any questions they may have.

Answers

1 **1** T (some children attend fee-paying schools but it is provided for everyone)
    2 T (some children are taught at home, but all children must have an education)
    3 T (students take GCSE exams at 16)
    4 F (most students pay for school meals, but they are free for children whose parents have a very low income)
    5 F (this is called 'corporal punishment' and has been illegal since 1987)
    6 F (this varies across the UK – usually, primary schools have bigger class sizes)
2 **1** start nursery school at 2 or 3
    2 start primary school at 4 or 5
    3 start secondary school at 11
    4 leave school at 16
    5 start university at any age but usually 18

3 Learners work in pairs to complete the school diary gap fill, using the words from the box. Go over the answers with the class. Discuss any points arising. Encourage learners to compare school times, school meal costs, after-school activities and term times with their countries.

Answers

3
1 16 **2** year **3** starts **4** club **5** rugby **6** party/disco **7** trip **8** disco/party

Extension

Learners research daily life in schools or at colleges and universities. At this level research work could be done from sites such as www.woodlands-junior.kent.sch.uk. Also learners can read the audio script and find out the answers to the following questions: the name of the exam British students take at 16 (GCSE); the name of the exam British students usually take at 18 (A Levels); the names of different university degrees and their different levels. Learners could do internet research to find out about schools in Wales, Northern Ireland and Scotland. *ESOL Activities Entry 1* and *Entry 2* provide further detailed information on education in the UK, with activities showing examples of timetables and typical subjects.

1 You are going to hear a teacher talking about education in British schools.

Are the statements below True (T) or False (F)? Circle the correct answer.

1 Education is free for children in the UK.   T/F

2 All children must go to school from 5 to 16.   T/F

3 Children must do exams at 16.   T/F

4 School dinners are free for everyone.   T/F

5 Teachers hit naughty children at school.   T/F

6 There are over 35 students in most classes.   T/F

2 **Read the sentences below about education in the UK. In pairs, guess the answers and write them in the boxes.**

		in England	in your country
1	The age children go to nursery school		
2	The age children start primary school		
3	The age children go to secondary school		
4	The age young people can leave school		
5	The age young people usually start university		

3 **Read the school diary below. Fill in the missing words from the box on the left.**

club

party   **disco**

rugby

starts

trip

year

16

Summerdale Secondary School

Diary for students from 11 to ¹ _____ **years old**

Holidays:
Christmas 17th Dec – 4th Jan; Easter 7th–22nd April; Summer 20th July – 7th Sept.

Terms:
There are three terms a ² _____ starting in September. School ³ _____ at 8.30 am and finishes at 3 pm.

Lunch:
1.30pm: Cost: £2.50 a day

Out of school activities: sports club, choir practice, tennis ⁴ _____ , guitar lessons, football and ⁵ _____ , modern dance.

Days on the school calendar: the Christmas ⁶ _____ , Year 11 ⁷ _____ to France, Sports Day, End of term ⁸ _____ !

13.2

Education in the UK

TYPE OF ACTIVITY
Reading and matching activity

LEVEL
Intermediate

TIME
45–60 minutes

AIMS
To explore developments in the British education system

VOCABULARY
apprenticeship, childcare, compulsory, faith school, lifelong learning, long-established, noble, nursery school, priest, private, provide, public, state education, tutor, wealthy

PREPARATION
One photocopy of worksheet for each pair of learners, cut into sets. Enlarged illustrations of classrooms from worksheet. Flip chart paper and pens.

Warmer

Display the images of the two classrooms and ask learners what they think each shows about changes in education (room set-up; one teacher standing at the front of the class, technology, punishment, etc.). Ask how they think the experience of going to school has changed. In pairs, learners think about how that compares with education today. Then they work in groups of 3–4 to brainstorm 'education' vocabulary. Pin these on the wall and discuss points arising as a class. For further awareness-raising and comprehension, teachers could use exercise 2 from Unit 13.1 (matching the correct name of the school to the age).

Tell learners that they're going to read about the British education system. Pre-teach any key vocabulary. Put learners in pairs/threes. Give learners a set of the cut-up texts. (Don't give them the cut-up headings yet.) Learners put the paragraphs in the correct order. Review the order as a class, reading through the paragraphs together and finding links within the text.

> **Answers**
>
> Paragraph links:
> From 1880 education was compulsory ... Nowadays education is free ... and compulsory
> In the state school system ... Although most British children go to state schools ...
> Many students then go on to university ... Although a lot of students want to go to university ... to train young people when they have started work ... It is very popular in the UK for adults to continue to do training ...

Give out sets of headings. Learners match them with the paragraphs. Then they reread the information and write one question from each card to ask another group. Check their work for accuracy while they're writing. Learners then sit in new groups and ask each other their questions. Alternatively, prepare some questions to ask the class. Arrange them in two teams and have a question and answer competition, awarding points for the first correct answers. Learners give their opinions on the following topics about education, in small groups or as a class debate.

- punishment in schools
- wearing a school uniform
- doing homework every night
- education in your country
- taking exams at school
- free education up to 16 years old
- learning by computer
- doing qualifications in your workplace
- university fees
- role of religion in education

Extension

To gain a better understanding of the education system, learners look up references to the words in *italics* on the Internet. Alternatively, ask the learners what they would like to find out more about and take in some appropriate reading material or information about the chosen topics from the Internet. There are more activities on the British education system in the UK in *ESOL Activities Entry 2* and *3*.

The history of education in the UK	It is said that the first school to open in Britain was at *Cor Tewdws* in Wales in 395 AD; Saint Augustine began a school in *Canterbury*, England in 597 AD. Early schools trained boys to be priests. Later, boys and girls of wealthy noble families were taught by private tutors. In the 14th century, public schools such as *Eton* gave free education to poor boys. From 1880, education was compulsory for children between 5 and 10.
When do you go to school?	Nowadays, education is free for everyone in the UK and is compulsory for children between 5 and 16. From the age of 3, children are also entitled to 2 days free nursery school a week. All state and most private schools follow the *National Curriculum,* which states which subjects may be studied at which time. In the state school system, most students take *GCSE* exams in a range of subjects at age 16. Many then take 3 to 6 *A and AS levels* at school or in 6th form colleges.
Public and private education	Although most British children go to state schools, some parents send their children to *independent* schools. The older, more famous schools are called *public schools* and the others *private schools*. Some children go to private *faith schools* run by religious groups. In both public and private schools, class sizes are usually small and children often live in school in term time. Many students then go on to university.
The Further Education route	Although a lot of students want to go to university, there are many others who prefer to learn a skill such as hairdressing, plumbing or cookery. They usually attend colleges of Further Education (FE colleges) and study *vocational courses*. There are also many *apprenticeship schemes*, especially in the building industry and trades, to train young people when they have started work.
Lifelong learning in the UK	It is very popular in the UK for adults to continue to do extra training when working or to study to acquire better qualifications at college. Sometimes this is called 'workplace training'. Also, many people attend evening classes in a range of subjects. They also take online courses, called distance learning, or even become *mature students* and take up a full-time university place or college training course.

13.3

TYPE OF ACTIVITY
Information exchange and word game

LEVEL
Advanced

TIME
50–60 minutes

AIMS
To gain an understanding of debates within British education

VOCABULARY
gap year, informal learning, the three Rs, upskill, vocational, GCSE

PREPARATION
One photocopy of the worksheet for each learner, cut into Parts A and B and word game. Flip chart paper and pens. Advanced dictionaries and some card or paper.

Learning for life

Warmer

Write *vocational skills* and *the three Rs* on the board. Ask learners what they think the session will be about (if they don't already know). Ask learners what these terms mean: *vocational skills* (practical learning/training such as plumbing or hairdressing), *the three Rs* (stands for **r**eading, w**r**iting and a**r**ithmetic). Ask learners what they would like to find out about the UK education system and write their questions on the board.

Form A/B pairs and give learners Card A or Card B and a dictionary. In their pairs, learners read their halves of the articles and check the vocabulary.

Copy the questions below. Give the A learners the questions for Part B and B learners the questions for Part A. Learners read these through. Learners make groups of four, two with text A and two with text B, and take it in turns to ask each other the questions and exchange answers. Go over all the answers with the class. Discuss any points arising. Learners compare British education with the system in their countries.

Questions for Part A

1 How many sounds are there in English?
2 What does 40% refer to?
3 What are the 'three Rs'?
4 Name a famous person who had dyslexia.
5 How have governments tried to improve literacy?
6 When did education become compulsory for 10-year-olds?
7 Name two key debates in education.

Questions for Part B

1 What do students do in a gap year?
2 When do students take GCSEs?
3 Name two kinds of vocational courses.
4 What has created the need for more academic qualifications?
5 What exam do students take at 6th form college?
6 What is a BSc?
7 Give two reasons why people do work-based training.

Answers to Part A

1 44 **2** the number of prisoners with severe dyslexia **3** reading, writing and arithmetic **4** Winston Churchill **5** by taking a more traditional approach to teaching and doing more testing **6** 1880 **7** the quality of teaching; the curricula; the acquisition of learning; who pays; poor literacy levels (two only needed)

Part B

1 have a year abroad **2** at 16 **3** catering, construction, IT, tourism, business (two only needed) **4** the need for a more highly skilled workforce; the decline of manufacturing industries **5** A or AS levels **6** Bachelor of Science degree **7** to upskill for their jobs; to be ready for future demands (21st century)

Focus learners on the vocabulary game *An Educated Guess!*. In teams of 3–4, learners choose four words on the topic of education and write the correct definition and two incorrect definitions on a piece of card as in the example. Each member of the team reads out the definitions to another team, who have to discuss the answers and guess the correct definition, e.g. text A: literacy, dyslexia, three Rs, curriculum; text B: gap year, vocational, upskill, fees. At the end of the game the learner with the highest score wins.

Extension

Learners discuss concerns they have about education. Prompt with references to topics in 13.2. They can research and debate key issues within the UK, or their own, education system.

A — Food for thought in British education

The routes of the education system

Education became compulsory for all children of between 5 and 10 in 1880 – a long time after Oxford (1167) and Cambridge (1209) had become the first major universities in Britain. There were few schools though free 'grammar' schools were introduced. Pupils followed a curriculum of Latin grammar, maths, astronomy and music. The selective system of grammar schools and secondary moderns was not superseded until the 1960s, when comprehensive education was introduced. Education is now a devolved issue and so varies in different areas of the UK.

The three 'R's

In modern Britain there are constant debates about education. They often centre on the quality and effectiveness of teaching and appropriate curricula, the acquisition of learning and who should pay for it. Nowadays there is a huge choice of courses and qualifications but a great concern is that some students leaving school at 16 are not competent in the 'three Rs' (reading, writing and arithmetic). Education is free up to the age of 18 but students have to borrow heavily to pay for degree courses.

Improving standards

To improve literacy and numeracy standards, recent governments have encouraged more traditional approaches to teaching, including more testing. Poor literacy is also related to social problems. For example, over 60% of prisoners in Britain's prisons have difficulty with literacy and numeracy and many are dyslexic.

Dyslexia and literacy

Dyslexia is quite widespread in the UK – some have suggested this is because of the complex relationship between English spelling and pronunciation (there are 44 sounds in English but only 26 letters). As a result, spelling can be problematic. One famous dyslexic, former Prime Minister Winston Churchill, who struggled at school, recognised that the English language was more powerful than military might and encouraged the spread of English language learning.

An educated guess!

dyslexia

When people can't eat they are suffering from dyslexia: false

Dyslexia is a sleeping disorder in old people: false

Dyslexia is a difficulty with reading/writing: TRUE

B — Learning for life

Educational drivers

As in many countries, the drive towards better qualifications with improved achievement in education has increased in Britain in recent decades. This is due in part to the need for a more highly skilled workforce that can compete effectively on an international level in the modern technological world. It is also because of the decline of manufacturing industries.

The British qualifications system

To mark the completion of compulsory education at 16, students usually take from five to ten GCSE exams (General Certificate of School Education). Many then continue into further education by enrolling on vocational courses in a college of further education. Here, students can learn practical skills including catering, construction, tourism, IT and business and can take appropriate qualifications up to degree level.

The university route

Students wishing to go to university will usually take three or four specific subjects at A (or AS) level, in school or at sixth form college. Under the British education system, young people tend to follow more specialist routes from age 16. They apply to their preferred university to do a degree, for example a BA (Bachelor of Arts) or a BSc (Bachelor of Science). Recently university fees have increased hugely, leading to concern that people from some backgrounds won't be able to afford it. Some students take a gap year to travel abroad and see the world, an experience often viewed as both educational and mind-expanding by potential future employers.

21st century skills

In the UK there are plenty of opportunities to continue education throughout one's life. It is now almost obligatory for employees to undertake further work-based training to upskill in their jobs and to equip themselves to deal with ever-changing demands in the 21st century.

An educated guess!

upskill

An upskill means a hard journey to take: false

To upskill means to train to a higher level: TRUE

Upskills are special workplace qualifications: false

Local arts and crafts

**TYPE OF
ACTIVITY**
Reading,
information search
and discussion

LEVEL
Elementary to Pre-
intermediate

TIME
40–50 minutes

AIMS
To look at British
creative arts at local
level

VOCABULARY
artist, artistic, arts
and crafts, bake,
creative, discount,
drum, drumming,
exhibition, explore,
glaze, hobby,
improve, leaflet,
pastime,
photography, pot,
pottery, produce,
session, taster,
throw, watercolour

PREPARATION
One photocopy of
the worksheet for
each learner.
Elementary
dictionaries. Display
pictures showing
different arts and
crafts.

Warmer

Write *pastimes* on the board and ask learners what it means. Learners work in pairs and write down any artistic/creative pastimes they think British people do in their free time. Alternatively, ask learners if they can tell you the names of the activities displayed around the room. Ask them which ones they think British people like doing.

> **Possible answers**
> drawing, calligraphy, dance (many types), drumming, knitting, fashion, film, jewellery/furniture/paper making, making clothes, music, painting, photography, pottery, sculpture, singing, weaving, writing

1 Give a copy of the worksheet to each learner. Read the introductory paragraph and look at the activities on the leaflet pages.

Give out dictionaries. Learners work in pairs/groups of three and do exercise 1, the vocabulary search. Go over answers with the class.

2 Focus learners on the comprehension questions. Go over the answers with the class. Discuss any points of interest.

> **Answers**
> 1 discount: lower price
>   workshop: informal, practical class
>   improve: get better
>   creative: artistic
>   session: one class or event
> 2
> 1 pottery for beginners (6–8 pm)
> 2 10.30 am–4 pm/£85
> 3 baking for pleasure, drumming workshop
> 4 10 am, £45
> 5 meet the tutors, get advice, try a taster session and get 10% discount on a course if you join

3 Learners do the discussion activity in small groups. Find out from the class what courses take place in their own countries, how popular they are and what learners have themselves done. Compare activities with those offered here. Ask why such activities are important and the value for different groups of people, e.g. the unemployed, women and children, older people.

Extension

Learners write a short paragraph on what they would like to study/what they like studying. They can include what else they would like to learn and say why they would enjoy this pastime. They can also complete a page for their British culture book/blog, adding visual examples of work produced in British evening/day classes.

In the UK, there are many ways people enjoy arts and crafts. Some go to exhibitions. Others like to go to evening classes and do art and crafts in their free time.

Every town and many villages have classes for people to attend. In the leaflet below you can read about the kinds of things British people often do through the year.

Creative Writing course

Writing can be lonely – but this course offers a relaxed place to share ideas and do fun activities to help you improve.

2 pm to 4 pm
8 Fridays,
starting
6th October
Cost: £50

Pottery for Beginners

Learn how to throw, glaze and fire a pot and much more!
6 pm to 8 pm
8 Wednesdays,
starting
4th October
Cost: £75

Working with Watercolours

A new class working with watercolours – we look at how to produce beautiful landscapes.
6 pm to 7.30 pm
8 Tuesdays, starting 3rd October
Cost: £65

Taster Day

Take this opportunity to come along to our FREE taster session and try out some of our activities on Sunday 1st September from 10 am–4 pm

• Meet the tutors
• Get advice on classes
• Have a taste of our wonderful courses and workshops

Special offer – come today and get 10% discount on courses if you join!

Baking for Pleasure

Enjoy bread-making for beginners

11 am to 3 pm, Saturday 15th December

Cost: £35

Street Dance

Enjoy a new music and dance event

10.00 am to 4.30 pm, Wednesday 18th January

Cost: £45

Drumming Workshop

Drumming workshop

Fun day for all – no experience needed

10 am to 3 pm, Sunday 2nd February

Cost: £35.00

Creative Photography weekend

The first of our three new photography weekends

10.30 am to 4 pm, Saturday 21st and Sunday 22nd February

Cost: £85.00

1 **What do these words mean?**

creative   discount   improve   session   workshop

2 **Work in pairs. Read the leaflets and answer the questions.**

1 What activity can people do on a Wednesday evening? ....
2 What time does the Creative Photography workshop start and finish? How much is it? ....
3 What courses can you do for under £40? ....
4 What time does the Street Dance day begin? How much is it? ....
5 What can you do on the Taster Day? ....

3 **Discuss the following questions in your groups.**

• What two activities you would like to try. Why would you like to do these?
• Tell each other about the pastimes people have in your country.
• Tell your group about your hobbies and interests.

14.2

British creative arts

TYPE OF ACTIVITY
Listening, matching and reading activity

LEVEL
Intermediate

TIME
50–60 minutes

AIMS
To explore some famous aspects of British cultural life

VOCABULARY
celebrated, costume, crafts, critic, fabulous, fascination, magician, moor, movement, novel, performer, poet laureate, romantic, scenery, sculpture, tragic

PREPARATION
One photocopy of the worksheet for each learner, enlarged and cut up into images, the listening and the readings. Option: take in more information about the artists on the work sheet.

Warmer

Write down the following on the board as a creative arts spidergram: *film and TV; art and sculpture; music and dance; writing and poetry; fashion and design.* Divide the class into groups. Learners write down any vocabulary they know, or famous British places or people associated with the titles on the sheets. Ask them to include ones related to their topic.

Suggested vocabulary

channel, documentary, episode (TV); band, concert, gig, play, production, orchestra, stage, theatre (dance, music, theatre); novel, poetry (writing); accessories, catwalk, design, model (fashion); display, easel, exhibition, gallery (the arts, sculpture and crafts)

Give out a copy of the worksheet and ask learners if they can identify them (Shakespeare's *Hamlet*; Brontë novel *Wuthering Heights*; *The Lord of the Rings* film poster). Find out what learners know about the stories. Ask learners which story appeals to them most, if they have seen the films or the play. See if they know when the stories were written, (Shakespeare's *Hamlet* around 1600, Emily Bronte's *Wuthering Heights* in 1847, JRR Tolkien's *Lord of the Rings* 1954).

▶ **60** Tell learners they're going to hear part of a radio show where people have to choose the music and book they take with them when they go on a long holiday. Play the audio while learners complete the chart. They check in pairs. Go over the answers with the class. Either at this stage or after the reading activity, learners interview each other on their own island choices.

Answers	
	The speaker
two records	Prokofiev's Suite Number 1 from *Romeo and Juliet*, David Bowie's *Heroes*
a favourite novel	Lord of the Rings
favourite poet (s)	Carol Ann Duffy, Benjamin Zephaniah
a favourite film	Slumdog Millionaire
a luxury item	Millais painting of Ophelia

Focus on the reading activity. Learners mark which people are mentioned in the audio (only Katherine Jenkins is not mentioned). Ask some information questions on the texts, e.g. *Name two poets/someone who enjoys travelling/two people born outside England*. Go over the answers with the class. Option: as a research activity, learners find out more about these contemporary artists and report their findings back to the class.

Extension

There is a range of ways to develop this unit. The stress of words and sentences in connected speech can be looked at in the audio. Film clips could be shown from *Wuthering Heights* looking at love and conflict; the *Lord of the Rings* looking at war and peace, human struggle; *Hamlet* in relationship to love, madness and betrayal. Learners could watch the film *Shakespeare in Love* and compare the role of women and men in society in 16th century compared with now.

Learners could also research some British creative talents such as Lily Allen, Billy Connolly, Judi Dench, Lenny Henry, Hilary Mantel, Helen Mirren, Ian McKellen, Alexander McQueen's fashion house, Harold Pinter, Vivienne Westwood. Early artists also of interest include the Pre-Raphaelite Brotherhood (founded by Dante Gabriel Rossetti, William Holman Hunt and John Everett Millais), the Brontë sisters (Anne, Charlotte and Emily), Jane Austen, World War I poets and artists.

O heavy burden!
5 POLONIUS
I hear him coming. Let's withdr
Enter Prince Hamlet   Exeu
HAMLET
10 To be, or not to be; that is the qu
Whether 'tis nobler in the mind to
The slings and arrows of outrageou
Or to take arms against a sea of tro
And, by opposing, end them. To die
No more, and by a sleep to sa

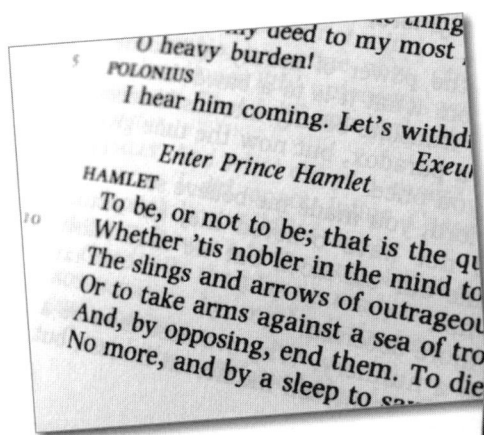

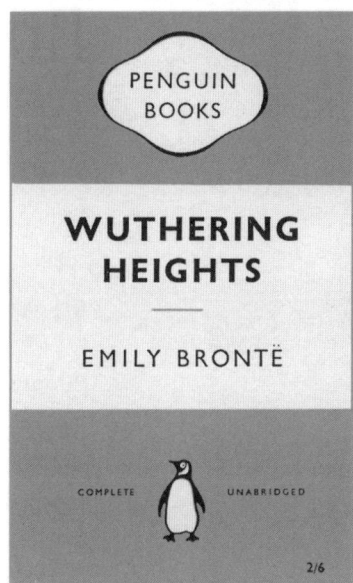

	The speaker	Yourself
two records		
a favourite novel		
favourite poet (s)		
a favourite film		
a luxury item		

Read the mini-biographies of some well-known, creative artists in Britain.

- Which artists are spoken about in the audio?
- Find out more about their lives and report this back to your class.

a

Benjamin Zephaniah was born in Birmingham, England. He is a very famous Rastafarian poet, writer, playwright and musician, and is a great traveller.

b

Katherine Jenkins is a Welsh mezzo-soprano singer. She is classically trained but performs a range of music including operatic arias, popular songs, musical theatre and hymns.

c

Carol Ann Duffy is the first British female Poet Laureate. She was born in Glasgow, Scotland, and studied philosophy before lecturing in poetry. She is celebrated for her fine poetry.

d

David Bowie was born in Brixton, London. A major figure for five decades in music, he's known as an innovative rock musician and record producer.

e

Danny Boyle was born in Manchester into an Irish Catholic family, and originally intended to be a priest. He's an unpredictable and exciting film director who made *Trainspotting* and *Slumdog Millionaire*.

f

Zadie Smith is a contemporary British writer. She was born in Brent, London to a Jamaican mother and an English father. Her most famous novel is called *White Teeth*.

14.3

British artistic achievement

TYPE OF ACTIVITY
Reading, listening and discussion

LEVEL
Advanced

TIME
50–60 minutes

AIMS
To explore trends in British art and popular culture

VOCABULARY
alternative, artwork, excerpt, installation, mainstream, performing poetry, rap, spray can, street art, work of art

PREPARATION
One photocopy of the worksheet for each learner. Advanced dictionaries. Produce a vocabulary matching activity from the text. Option: pictures of the artists' work for exercise 3.

Warmer

Learners work in pairs. Ask them to write a definition for the term *popular culture*. Discuss their responses with the class. Check a dictionary for a formal definition. Then learners list cultural activities or fields included in popular culture. Contrast this with '*high*' *culture*. Elicit the names of famous British artists, designers, filmmakers, art movements and write these on the board. Discuss responses with the class.

Suggested categories

'**High**' **culture:** architecture, ballet, classical and mainstream theatre, gold and silversmithing, landscape painting, opera, poetry and writing, photography, science, sculpture

Popular culture: alternative books, circus, crafts (e.g. knitting), film and video, jazz, blues, 'pop' and rock music, musicals, rap and performing poetry, installations, street art, fashion, street dance, TV and radio, writing,

Both: dance, mainstream/popular music, painting, sculpture, theatre

1   Tell learners they're going to read about UK popular culture. Give a copy of the worksheet to each learner. Learners read the article once and underline new vocabulary, then check in pairs. Alternatively, give out a vocabulary activity produced prior to the class (e.g. a definition matching activity, a true/false definition activity, a sentence gap fill). Go over new vocabulary with the class.

2   Learners answer the questions (1–4). Go over the answers with the class. Encourage learners to discuss their ideas in more depth. Ask them what the text suggests and how this picture compares with their country.

> **Answers**
>
> 1   The conservative values of a class-ridden world
> 2   urban rebelliousness, defiance, belligerence, rowdiness, a tendency to bullishness
> 3   Prime Minister's Question Time in Parliament and Saturday night intoxication in cities
> 4   the drive to challenge: root out hypocrisy, licence and self-satisfaction

3   ▶ 61 Tell learners they are going to listen to a critic discussing modern British art, from the 1990s onwards. Ask them if they recognise the two artists shown, but do not check answers. Play the audio for learners to complete the table with the names of the artists and one of their artworks. Learners identify the two artists shown (Grayson Perry and Banksy). Go over the answers with the class. If available, show learners pictures of the other artists' work. The two artworks shown on the page are *We've Found the Body of Your Child* (Grayson Perry) and *Sweeping It Under the Carpet* (Banksy). Discuss the work and explore their views on these works of art in more depth.

> **Answers**
>
> | Artist | Work mentioned |
> | --- | --- |
> | Tracey Emin | My bed |
> | Damien Hirst | For the love of God |
> | Grayson Perry | Grecian-like urns, images of car wrecks and mobile phones |
> | Banksy | Sweeping It Under the Carpet, Kissing policemen |
> | Anish Kapoor | Orbit Tower, paint cannon |
>
> The critic thinks that British art has been innovative and ground breaking in recent decades, especially since the arrival of New Brit Art in the 90s.

Extension

Learners do some internet research on modern British artists, artistic movements and popular culture. Look at the websites for the Tate Modern Gallery, Edinburgh Festival, Brighton Festival and newspaper arts pages, e.g. *The Guardian*, *The Telegraph*. Learners report back to the class. Alternatively, learners give presentations, with slides, on their favourite modern British artist, art movement or a popular, cultural activity.

1 Read the article below, describing the influences shaping popular British culture. Underline new vocabulary and discuss their meanings with a partner.

Popular culture unwrapped

In recent decades, there has been a blossoming of creative energy and exploration in popular culture. From the flamboyant Edwardian look of a 1950s teddy boy to the haunting stare of the 1990s Goth, popular, grass-roots culture has confronted and swept aside the conservative values of a traditional, class-ridden world, replacing it with a model that refuses to conform to the social and creative mores of earlier, more elitist times.

The shift in British creative direction also highlights the underlying national characteristics of defiance and belligerence. This urban rebelliousness could be observed in London a few years ago when David Blaine spent 44 days suspended in a glass box in London without food. Instead of the admiration he received from crowds in America, here he was met with jeering, mischievous crowds and pelted with eggs and cabbages – the tradition missiles of a medieval London mob.

Not comfortable viewing, but interesting if considered as mob defiance to a pretentious member of the 'intellectual elite.' But where else do the roots of this modern British rowdiness lie? Well, probably in all aspects of British culture and society – look no further than Parliament and the televised Prime Minister's Question Time or the Saturday night displays of intoxication in our towns and cities. It is all part of a complex British cultural inheritance, a lack of conformity to the European norm, a tendency to bullishness and a challenge to the ruling class, all captured so aptly in the cartoons of the 18th century political and social satirist, William Hogarth.

Ultimately, the British find little need to praise and parody the 'Great and the Good'. They prefer to dig cynically at society's heart and root out hypocrisy, licence and self-satisfaction with an even hand. It is this drive to challenge that feeds creative minds and from which springs innovation and cultural growth in the UK.

2 Answer the following questions.

1 According to the author, what has been challenged by popular British culture?

2 What typical British behaviour does the author illustrate? Do you agree with her view?

3 What aspects of British society reflect rowdy behaviour?

4 What does the writer suggest encourages creativity in the UK?

3 Listen to the audio discussing the importance of five British artists. As you listen, write in the artists' names and one of their artworks below.

Artist	Work mentioned

- What does the speaker think is modern Britain's contribution to the world of art?
- What do you think in general of the work of the artists mentioned?
- What are your views on modern art and art movements in general?

15.1

Where people live

TYPE OF ACTIVITY
Listening and information gathering

LEVEL
Elementary to Pre-intermediate

TIME
40–50 minutes

AIMS
To find out about types of housing in the UK

VOCABULARY
accommodation, avenue, block of flats, bungalow, buy, cottage, drive, lane, place, rent, semi-detached house, terraced house,

PREPARATION
One photocopy of the worksheet and one copy of the audio script for each learner.

Warmer

Ask learners what they know about housing in the UK. Prompt with: *Do British people buy or rent houses? Do most British people have gardens? Do people take showers or baths? Do most houses have gas or electricity? Do British people like pets? If so, where do they live? Can you think of any other words for 'houses' and 'roads'?* (see examples below). Alternatively, make a questionnaire for learners to discuss in pairs. Read out the information below.

How people live in the UK: Most British families (70%) want to buy houses – they don't really like living in flats. Students and young people mostly rent accommodation. Many people have gardens and some have allotments (areas of land they rent cheaply from the council to grow food). In the past, the British only had baths but now most people have showers, or both. Most houses and flats have gas and electricity. Many people own pets – usually cats, dogs, hamsters, rabbits, budgies or fish – and they normally live inside, but rabbits usually live outside.

Types of accommodation: bungalow, cottage, country house, flat (US apartment), detached/semi-detached house, stately home, terraced house
Road names: avenue, close, crescent, drive, lane, mews, parade, passage, place, road, street

1   Give a worksheet to each learner. Learners work in pairs to match the types of house with the pictures. Go over the answers with the class.

Answers

1 a block of flats   **2** a semi-detached house   **3** a cottage   **4** a bungalow
5 a terraced house   **6** a country house

Focus learners on the text. Read the paragraph about housing in the UK. Discuss the information, asking learners if it is the same in their country.

2   ▶ 62–67
Option 1: listening for information (suitable for stronger learners)
Tell learners they're going to hear people talking about where they live. Look at the information needed to complete the boxes together. Play the audio for learners to complete the table. Learners check answers in pairs. Play the audio again and go over the answers. Alternatively, set up a jigsaw listening activity for learners. Give pairs of learners alternate numbers to complete (1, 3, 5 and 2, 4, 6). Learners exchange information to complete the chart.

Option 2: milling practice (suitable for less strong learners)
Use the questionnaire as a milling practice. Enlarge the table and give each learner a copy. Then give out a cut-up copy of the audio (1–6) to each group of six learners. Learners first fill in the information on their table, then exchange information with their group. Play the audio for learners to check their answers.

Answers

1	Raymond	cottage	3	Rose Cottage, Mill Lane, Coleraine, Northern Ireland
2	Gareth and Megan	bungalow	2	12, Southwood Close, Denby, Wales
3	Holly and Amos	flat	2	Flat 32, Weston Court, Peckham, London
4	Jamie	terraced house	1	4, Mill Street, Edinburgh, Scotland
5	Lady Searle	country house	9	Crestley House, Little Beading, Kent
6	Sirus and Aruna	semi-detached house	4	16, The Drive, Birmingham B12 7RU

Extension

Learners use a similar chart to find out information about their classmates' accommodation. Instead of asking about addresses, an option would be to ask about gas, electricity, gardens, pets, etc.

1 What kind of house do you live in? Match the names of houses with the pictures below.

block of flats   bungalow   cottage   country house   semi-detached house   terraced house

Houses in the UK

Britain is quite small but it has a big population of over 60 million people. You can see many different types of houses in the UK. In towns and cities, people often live in terraced, or semi-detached, houses, and flats. In the countryside, many people live in villages in old-style houses, small, traditional cottages or bungalows. There are lots of farms and beautiful country houses here too.

2 You are going to hear some people talking about where they live. Listen to the audio. Fill in the information in the boxes below.

	Names	Type of accommodation	Number of bedrooms	Address
1				
2				
3				
4				
5				
6				

15.2

Home sweet home

TYPE OF ACTIVITY
Reading and discussion

LEVEL
Intermediate

TIME
50–60 minutes

AIMS
To find out about British homes

VOCABULARY
back-to-back, buyer, estate agent, house, housing estate, mortgage, pond, poverty, row, terraced house, timeline, thatched cottage, utility services, Brit, Tudor house/Georgian house, the Industrial Revolution

PREPARATION
One photocopy of the worksheet for each learner.
Pictures of UK houses from lesson 15.1.

Warmer

Ask learners what they know about British homes and housing. Write their comments on the board, e.g. *people like to own homes, they mostly have showers and central heating, people like old style houses with gardens and pay lots of money for them*. Show pictures of houses from lesson 15.1 for them to identify, e.g. semi-detached, terraces, bungalow.

1 Tell learners they are going to find out more about housing in Britain. Give a copy of the worksheet to each learner. Focus on the first paragraph. They read the article and underline the different styles of housing mentioned in the text. Working in pairs, write a timeline with dates and notes underneath, explaining the developments through the centuries. (16th C … 17th C …18th C …19th C …) Option: write a timeline on the board and complete it as learners feed back. Discuss the development of facilities and utilities within homes.

2 Learners read the second and third paragraphs and answer the questions, checking in pairs. Go over answers with the class. Discuss any points arising, e.g. the national interest in DIY. Find out if this is similar in their countries.

3 Focus on the third paragraph. Learners read the text again, turn it over and tell their partners what they remember. Learners then answer the question. Go over their responses with the class and deal with points arising.

4 Learners do exercise 4, marking different buildings on the map (Tudor, Georgian, Victorian, etc.). Go over the answers with the class, referring back to visual examples of each, if available. Discuss what learners imagine life would have been like for the different classes in society (upper, middle, working class) and the differences between town and country people's lives.

5 Learners work together on the discussion questions in exercise 5.

> **Answers**
> 1 learners write short summaries covering 16th century (Tudor); 18th century (Georgian); 19th century (Regency/Victorian); 20th century
> 2 **1** Do It Yourself house decoration and repairs; they have respect for the amateur and like to 'have a go' **2** they have more character **3** barns, windmills, old churches, train stations, lighthouses
> 3 they have working chimneys and fireplaces but use central heating; bathrooms often have two taps with hot and cold water, not a mixer tap; often showers are on top of baths; cats and dogs sleep inside the homes
> 4 **a** modern bungalows **b** thatched cottages **c** a church **d** Georgian shops **e** Victorian terraces **f** a windmill

Extension

Learners can research the National Trust website for information about the National Trust charity. The teacher sets questions for them to answer, e.g. *Who set up the NT? When and why was it started? How many people are members now? How much land does the NT own? How many properties do they own?* Go over the answers with the class. Discuss the value of this kind of organisation to a country, its environment and heritage.

Learners can also research styles of architecture and housing in towns and villages on the Internet to add to their British culture book/blog. Example places of interest might include: Bath, Knaresborough, Ludlow, Royal Tunbridge Wells, Skipton, New Forest (England); Ballycastle (Northern Ireland); Aberystwyth, Portmeirion, St David's (Wales); Glasgow, Tobermory (Scotland). Learners could then give mini-presentations about the places they have researched, with visuals. The whole class could produce a timeline of places with information and visuals on it about the buildings they have explored and the styles described in the lesson.

House styles

In the UK people often describe houses by their style at the time they were built. For example, 15th and 16th century buildings with thatched roofs, white painted fronts with black, wooden timbers are known as Tudor buildings, after the Tudor kings and queens. In the early 18th century, neo-classical, pillared houses were called Georgian in style, after the kings George I–IV. Then came the elegant, bow-windowed Regency crescents and terraces of the mid-1800s.

Later in the 19th century, when Victoria was queen, the Industrial Revolution began. Britain suddenly saw a huge increase in the urban population. In some cities, up to ten people lived in a single room, in terrible poverty. As a result, rows of small, back-to-back houses were built, known as Victorian terraces. Gas and electricity were later introduced and the use of phones became more widespread in the early 20th century.

Inside British houses

People like their homes to look stylish and modern and property owners spend thousands of pounds on fitted kitchens and bathrooms and put down wooden flooring or fitted carpets. House interiors vary a lot but there are some unusual differences to other countries. Many homes still have working chimneys and fireplaces – even though people use central heating. In bathrooms you'll often find two taps with hot and cold water, rather than a mixer tap, and showers are often fitted on top of baths. In many homes you'll see computers, large TV screens sharing space with old books and ornaments – ideally there's a cat or dog curled up on the sofa or lying cosily by the fireplace!

Modern homes

Most British people dream of owning their own home, whether it's a modern purpose-built flat, a Victorian terrace or a bungalow. They borrow huge amounts of money (called mortgages) from banks to do so. Old-style houses are seen by the British as having more 'character' than new properties and people convert any buildings into dwellings, from barns and windmills to old churches, train stations and lighthouses.

TV programmes about gardening, DIY (Do-It-Yourself house decoration and repairs) and moving home are very popular and many Brits decorate their houses and do gardening in their free time. People have a lot of respect for the amateur and enjoy 'having a go' at things.

1 Describe the changes in British housing over the centuries on a timeline with information on dates and styles.

2 Answer the following questions
  1 What is DIY? Why do the British like to do this?
  2 Why do British people like old houses?
  3 What unusual places do people live in?

3 What differences can you find in British homes compared to those overseas?

4 Write in the names of the types of buildings found in the village below (a–f).

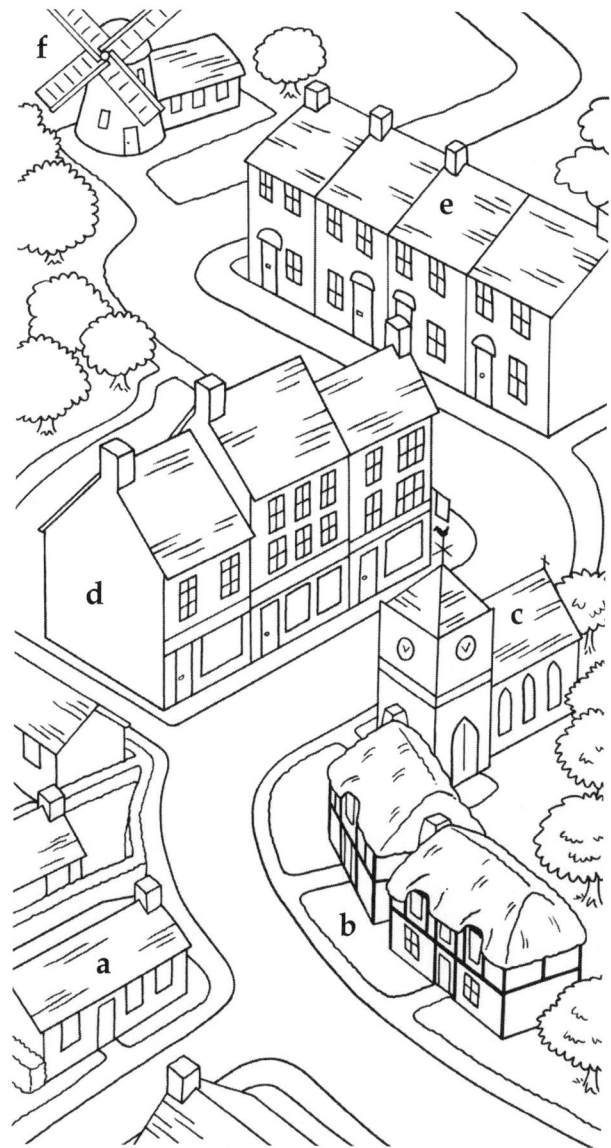

5 Discuss the following questions in your groups.
  • What is your opinion of houses and flats in the UK?
  • Describe your own house to your group.
  • What do you think houses will look like in the future?

15.3

TYPE OF ACTIVITY
Reading and discussion

LEVEL
Advanced

TIME
50–60 minutes

AIMS
To gain an understanding of British housing issues

VOCABULARY
council housing, eco-housing, franchised, home owner, legitimate, private sector, public sector, utility service, tenancy, vendor, vulnerable

PREPARATION
One photocopy of the worksheet for each pair of learners, cut into sets.

British housing issues

Warmer

Write up the unit title, *British housing issues*. Ask learners what topics it might include. Write their responses on the board, e.g. *modern housing, cost of buying/renting, interior design, cost of utilities, space*. Ask them what services or facilities might be included under the heading *Local community services*. Prompt with *council services* and *utilities*.

> **Possible answers**
> **British housing issues** house/flat, own/rent accommodation, social housing, eco-housing, lack of housing, mortgages, utility costs and bills
> **Community services** local services include rubbish collection, recycling, emergency services, maintenance of roads, libraries, some crèche, some public transport
> **Utilities** water, gas and electricity supply are private (but the national electricity grid is publicly owned). Public transport – trains, buses and coaches – are now owned by, or franchised to, private companies. The London Underground is publicly owned.

Tell learners they're going to read some information on UK housing issues. Give a set of reading cards and visuals to each pair. Learners skim read each section and match the pictures with the paragraphs. They then put the cards in the correct sequence. (Cohesion links in vocabulary and contexts: housing ... problem ... attempt to solve housing shortage; local councils ... councils are also responsible; homelessness ... homeless). Feed back.

Give out the questionnaires to pairs of learners for them to find the answers in the text. Go over the answers with the class.

> **Answers**
> **A** Housing options **B** Housing support **C** Community in progress **D** The Big Issue
> **1** *at a premium*: expensive and sought after; *the housing ladder*: the route upwards when buying bigger and bigger properties; *a catchment area*: the area in which something is served or contained; *vulnerably housed*: people whose living accommodation is not settled or permanent
> **2** by giving the opportunity to earn a legitimate weekly income and offering support, advice and guidance
> **3** a tax based on the size of the property and the catchment area
> **4** In the UK renting is expensive, taking a large part of incomes whereas in some other countries in Europe it's cheaper, more common (widespread) and greater tenancy protection exists
> **5** by offering traditional, low-rental council housing, affordable housing within private building projects, publicly supported, environmentally friendly, social housing projects
> **6** refuse clearance, road maintenance and drains, libraries and public spaces and part fund the police, fire and healthcare services

Draw a pie chart on the board showing 32% of people own outright (including retired people); 37% of the population have a mortgage (the largest of all percentages); 18% rent from the local authority; 13% of people rent privately.

Emphasise that 70% of people in the UK buy their own property. Discuss with learners the advantages of buying your own home (e.g. it's yours to decorate and live in as you want, it's an investment) and the disadvantages (e.g. cost, sometimes couples lose their homes if they separate or if they can't afford payments, difficulty of moving if you change jobs). Then learners work together on the discussion questions.

Extension

Learners can research different aspects of housing in the UK in more depth (e.g. eco buildings, modern architecture, 'north–south' divide (differences in costs and quality of housing), city versus village life and the development of utility services in Britain). Learners could write a report on their findings, comparing these figures with their own countries. Alternatively, this could be delivered in presentation form to the class or as a short reportage as a video or class blog.

Housing options in the UK ...

In recent decades, housing has been a constant problem. This has been in part because the UK is relatively small and building land is at a premium. The price of buying or renting property has also rocketed. For example, the cost of an average 2-bedroomed house in 1987 was £40,000. By 2010 it was £140,000. This has made house buying extremely expensive. As a consequence, a huge percentage of a person's income is taken up in mortgage payments or rent. This contrasts with some other countries in Europe where rents are often cheaper and greater tenancy protection is in place.

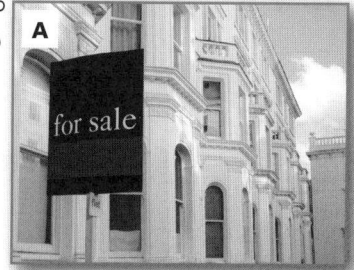

Housing support

In an attempt to solve the housing shortage, governments have put in place a range of support options for low-income families unable to get on the housing ladder, as well as the elderly, single parents and the disabled. These include traditional, low-rental council housing; affordable housing within private building projects; publicly supported, environmentally friendly, social housing projects. In addition, local councils provide publicly funded, emergency housing for families in crisis and other vulnerable groups.

Community in progress – who pays?

Local councils are responsible for a range of services including refuse clearance, road maintenance and drains, libraries and public spaces. They also partly fund the police, fire and healthcare services. To pay for these, people pay Council Tax, based on the size of the property they own or rent and their catchment area. A two-bedroomed flat for example, could cost between £600 to over £1,000 a year depending on its location. These issues perhaps seem less important when compared to another concern in Britain – homelessness.

The Big Issue – a hand up, not a hand out

To help alleviate the problems of the homeless, John Bird and Gordon Roddick set up _The Big Issue_. This weekly entertainment and current affairs magazine offers homeless and vulnerably housed people the opportunity to earn a weekly income. Homeless people sell the magazine on the streets. It costs £2.50 and vendors keep £1.25 of every sale. The charity believes that earning an income is the first step on the journey away from homelessness. It works exclusively with vendors, offering support, advice and guidance.

Housing Questionnaire

1 **Below are several expressions from the text. What do they mean?**

at a premium   catchment area   the housing ladder   vulnerably housed

2 **How does _The Big Issue_ help homeless people?**

3 **What is Council Tax and how are Council Tax payments decided?**

4 **What are the differences between Britain and other countries in rented accommodation?**

5 **How do local councils support vulnerable groups?**

6 **What services do local councils provide?**

Discuss the following questions in your groups.

- What are the similarities and differences in accommodation between your country and the UK?

- What are the best aspects of housing in your country?

- What housing problems does your country have?

- How do you think homelessness can be solved in modern society?

- What are the concerns facing housing in the future?

- Describe your home or your ideal house to your group.

People in the law

TYPE OF ACTIVITY
Reading and information search

LEVEL
Elementary to pre-intermediate

TIME
46–50 minutes

AIMS
To find out about key professionals in the British legal system

VOCABULARY
break the law, court, crime, criminal, detective, guilty, judge, jury, law, legal, local, magistrate, officer, ordinary, plain clothes, police, punishment, rob, steal, uniform, CID

PREPARATION
One set of reading cards for each pair of learners and a set of elementary dictionaries. Flip chart paper and pens.

Warmer

Tell learners they're going to read about British law. Write up the phrase *to break the law* and check that they understand it. Ask them if they can name the people who break the law, e.g. *thief, robber, criminal, drug dealer, kidnapper*. Write their responses on the board. Then ask them to name some jobs people do around the law, e.g. police officer, *detective, inspector, judge, lawyer, barrister, solicitor*) and where they work, e.g. *court/courtroom, police station, the street*.

Give a set of information cards to each group of four learners. Learners read the information and headings and match the pictures with the information cards. Option: cut the questions from cards and ask learners to match these with cards A–D. Go over the answers with the class. Alternatively, give out a previously prepared definition and matching vocabulary activity. After learners have completed this, give out the sets of information cards for learners to continue with the activity.

Learners read the information cards and answer the questions together, using dictionaries if necessary. Go over the answers with the class. Go through each card and compare the British system with that in their countries, as appropriate. Ask them what the crime problems are in their country, e.g. *drugs, theft, car crime*.

Answers

A The British Police
B The lawyers
C The magistrates and judges
D The jury

A 1 Robert Peel started the police force
   2 dark blue uniforms and hats
   3 investigate who committed a crime
B 1 civil and criminal courts
   2 a person who gives advice to people and works in a civil court
   3 work for a person who has to go to a criminal court, or someone taking a person to court
C 1 decide punishments for small crimes
   2 they are not paid
   3 control the courtroom and decide the punishment
D 1 a group of 12 ordinary people
   2 to decide if people are guilty or not guilty
   3 they are not paid

Extension

Learners research a famous UK crime story or character (real or fiction). Suggested people: Burke and Hare, Jack the Ripper, the Kray twins (real); Robin Hood, Sweeney Todd (legendary); Writers and their characters: Agatha Christie (Hercule Poirot, Miss Marple), Arthur Conan Doyle (Sherlock Holmes), Ian Fleming (James Bond). Learners could also write a short biography on their story or character to deliver to the class.

A

The British police

In 1850 Robert Peel started a police force in London because there were so many robberies in the streets. The policemen, called 'Bobbies' by the local people, were the first of their kind in the world.

Today, in the modern police service there are two types of British police officers. In the streets you can see policemen and women in dark blue uniforms and hats who try to stop crimes. Other officers wear plain clothes and are called detectives – they try to find out who is guilty of a crime.

1 What happened in 1850?

2 What do the police wear?

3 What do detectives do?

B

The lawyers

In England and Wales there are two kinds of courts: civil courts for small crimes and criminal courts for serious crimes. When people have a legal problem, they usually talk to a solicitor to get advice. They also work for people in civil courts. The lawyers who work in criminal courts are called barristers.

Some barristers work for the person who has to go to court. Others work for someone who is taking another person to court. In Scotland and Northern Ireland the system is different.

1 What are the two kinds of courts?

2 What is a solicitor?

3 What do barristers do?

C

The magistrates and judges

Most men and women who live in Welsh and English towns or cities can become *magistrates* (or a Justice of the Peace in Scotland). They sit in *magistrates courts* and, like judges, decide the punishments for small crimes and problems. They do not get paid but get a lot of training to do this important job.

Judges work in crown courts. They are in control of the courtroom. If the jury says that a person is guilty, the judge must decide the punishment.

1 What do magistrates do?

2 How much are they paid?

3 What do judges do?

D

The jury

In England and Wales, serious crimes are tried in crown courts, in front of a judge and jury. A jury is a group of twelve ordinary men and women from the local town or city. In court, they cannot ask questions but must listen to the evidence from both sides. Their job is to decide if a person is guilty or not guilty.

The jury does not get paid but they get a small amount of money for each day they are away from work.

1 What is a jury?

2 What is their job?

3 How much are they paid?

Law in the UK

TYPE OF ACTIVITY
Reading and discussion

LEVEL
Intermediate

TIME
50–60 minutes

AIMS
To explore aspects of British law

VOCABULARY
adopt, commit a crime, court, crime, criminal, cruel, (dis)honest, endemic, investigate, keep an eye on, legal system, on duty, police force, relatively, scary, statement, surveillance, widely, CCTV

PREPARATION
One photocopy of the worksheet for each learner.

Warmer

Tell learners they're going to find out about the law in the UK. Write the first two or three letters of a word associated with crimes on the board, e.g. *ro.....* (*robber*); *mug.....* (*mugger*); *mur.....* (*murderer*); *te.....* (*terrorist*); *ki.....* (*kidnapper*). Learners work in pairs and can use dictionaries. Alternatively, give them two minutes to write down the names of as many kinds of crimes and criminals as possible, e.g. *arson/to commit arson/an arsonist, kidnapping/to kidnap/a kidnapper, killing/to kill/a killer, murder/to murder/a murderer, robbery/to rob/a robber, shoplifting/to shoplift/a shoplifter, theft/to thieve/a thief, terrorism/a terrorist.*

A Give a copy of the worksheet to each pair of learners. Learners read the questionnaire and circle their answers. Then they discuss their responses in pairs/groups. Go over the answers with the class. Learners look at the 'good or bad law' boxes and give their opinion. Discuss each law with the class, encouraging learners to make comparisons with their own countries.

> **Answers**
> **1** T **2** F (but you can do some part-time work) **3** T (but they have to have a reason, e.g. a light that isn't working) **4** F (this is called bigamy and you can go to prison for this) **5** F (you can only be held for 24 hours by the police without a charge; with special permission it can be for up to seven days without a charge, e.g. for terrorism suspects) **6** T **7** T **8** T **9** F (except in certain locations such as airports and railway stations) **10** T

B Focus learners on the three pictures. Ask them what the signs are. Learners read the article on crime in the UK. Ask them information questions about the text and discuss the effectiveness of these forms of crime prevention (suggestions below).

> **Possible questions and answers**
> How many times a day are people in London caught on CCTV cameras? (150)
> How does the Neighbourhood Watch scheme work? (Neighbours try to look after each others' homes and properties)
> Why are people more afraid of crime in Britain? (due to new types of electronic crime, the way crime is reported on TV and news coverage and detective programmes)

Learners compare this information with their own countries. Draw out a discussion on the use of CCTV, privacy, crime and fear, modern crimes compared to times past.

Focus learners on *How honest are you?* Learners complete the questionnaire in pairs. Discuss their responses with the class. Find out what they consider to be honest or dishonest. Ask what is important and not so important on the list.

Extension

Set up a semi-formal debate. Find out what topics learners would like to discuss, e.g. *CCTV should be banned from most streets and inside buildings; Cigarettes should be banned; People should be allowed to have more than one wife or husband.* Explain the rules to the class. Divide learners into groups of four and give them a debate topic. Tell learners to develop their arguments, with two people for the proposal and two against it. Pairs of learners prepare their arguments. Each pair of learners then puts their views and arguments forward, for and against their proposal. The debate is then open for everyone to ask questions. Finally the teacher counts hands to decide which pair has won the debate. (Teams vote on the best debaters, not just reflecting their own view.)

Alternatively, ask learners if they know of any British TV programmes about the law, or any famous detectives from TV programmes or books, e.g. Sherlock Holmes, Poirot, Inspector Morse, The Bill. Find out their opinions of these.

A What do you know about British law?

1 Read the statements in the box below about British laws. In pairs, decide if you think the statements are true or false.

	True/False?	Good law?	Bad law?
1 It is illegal for teenagers under 18 to buy alcohol or cigarettes.	T/F		
2 If you are 14 you can do full-time work.	T/F		
3 The police can stop you in your car at any time.	T/F		
4 You can have more than one wife or husband in the UK.	T/F		
5 The police can hold you for three days before charging you.	T/F		
6 If you are cruel to an animal you can go to prison.	T/F		
7 If you want to work with children you must first have a police check.	T/F		
8 You can be sent to prison for not paying your tax.	T/F		
9 British police carry guns when on duty.	T/F		
10 It is illegal to use a mobile phone while driving.	T/F		

2 Read the boxes again and tick the box to say whether you think the laws are good or bad. Discuss your answers with your partner. Ask why they have this opinion.

B Crime in the UK

Britain today is actually a relatively safe place compared to the past. And, compared to some countries, people have a relatively good relationship with the police. However, people often say that the *fear* of crime has increased. This may be because of new types of electronic crime, the way crime is reported by newspapers and on TV and the number of frightening detective programmes.

Nowadays the police and the general public adopt many new ways to prevent crime. For example, there are around 150,000 Neighbourhood Watch schemes in Britain, where people keep an eye on their neighbours' property. New technology is also widely used. There are over 2 million CCTV cameras in Britain – about one for every 32 people, each person is caught on camera about 50 times a day. Britain is in fact one of the top five countries in the world using 'endemic surveillance' of its people. However, in 2008, it was revealed that only 3% of street robberies in London were solved using CCTV images.

You are on CCTV

This is a NEIGHBOURHOOD WATCH AREA

LOCAL POLICE INFORMATION
CRIME HOTSPOT
Thieves are currently operating in this area

How honest are you?

- Would you download music illegally from the Internet?
- Would you pretend not to know the traffic laws in a foreign country – even if you did?
- Would you take pens or paper from work to use at home?
- Would you watch illegally produced film DVDs at home?
- Would you tell a shop assistant if he or she gave you too much change?
- Would you try not to pay your full amount of tax?
- Have you answered all these questions honestly?

16.3

TYPE OF ACTIVITY
Listening for information and discussion

LEVEL
Advanced

TIME
50–60 minutes

AIMS
To gain an understanding of the development and structure of British legal system

VOCABULARY
advocate, civil court, civil liberties, criminal court, crown court, deport, disability, disabled, fate, feral, human rights, legal system, legislation, magistrates' court, nag, outcast, plunge, sentence, youth court, BME (black and minority ethnic) groups

PREPARATION
One photocopy of the worksheet for each learner, cut into sets of question cards for groups of learners. Option: cut the discussion sections from the worksheet into strips; flip chart paper and pens.

Legal concerns

Warmer

Tell learners that you are going to look at the legal system and punishment in the UK. In pairs/groups, learners write words or expressions on the topic of the law on the board. Highlight two or three words below and ask learners to write definitions. Elicit some examples from the class. Learners look up the dictionary definitions and see how similar their definitions are.

Possible vocabulary
adversarial system, appeal, acquit someone, barrister, criminal investigation, civil liberty, criminal offence, defence, evidence, pass sentence, prosecutor, trial by jury, verdict

Part A
1   Give a copy of the worksheet to each learner. Focus on the pictures. Ask what they show and the context (all are associated with policing, punishment or control). In pairs, learners match and label the pictures. Discuss briefly the changes in acceptable forms of punishment through the ages.

2   Focus on the pre-listening question. Ask learners to discuss the punishments in pairs and write down a few notes on these. Tell them that they're going to hear a talk about law and punishment. Learners write notes on the audio, write their responses on the board.

3   ▶ 68   Play Part 1 of the audio and answer the true/false questions. Go over the answers with the class. Discuss any points arising with the group (highlight policing of demonstrations, tagging and civil rights).

Answers
1 d   2 e   3 a   4 b   5 c
2 1 the Old Bailey: the Central Criminal Court in England   2 kettling: used by the police to contain a crowd within a limited area from 1999   3 a transportation ship: going to Australia until 1868   4 the pillory: a form of punishment used up to late 18th century where men were whipped   5 an electronic tag: used to monitor people on curfew or house arrest
3 1 F (they were outcasts)   2 T   3 T   4 F (up to the 1860s)

Part B
▶ 69   Focus on Part 2 of the listening. Learners read through the questions on the worksheet, listen to the discussion and answer the questions, then check answers in pairs. Play the audio again. Go over answers with the class, discussing the advantages and disadvantages of recent legislation in Britain.

Answers
4 1   women, BME (black and minority ethnic groups), disabled, gays and lesbians, individuals
2   the government brought in some strict new regulations, holding people longer without trial, house arrest and tagging for instance
3   kettling in demonstrations, the proliferation of CCTV, electronic tagging
4   people complain they have little or no control over regulations imposed on us from Brussels

Learners do the discussion in groups of four. Option: give out sets of previously cut up questions (add more as relevant to the class). Place them upside down on the tables. Learners turn the questions over one at a time and discuss them. Go over any points arising with the class.

Extension

Find out what aspects of law learners are interested in. Ask them in what way our lives today have benefited from past laws and ask what future laws we might benefit from. Set up a formal debate using some of the issues raised, e.g. terrorism versus civil rights, the right to demonstrate, concerns about CCTV surveillance and videoing citizens, bugging, intercepting of emails/phone calls.

A Legal rights and wrongs

1 Look at the pictures on the right. Label the pictures (a–e) with the titles (1–5).

1 The Old Bailey (London's Criminal Justice Court) ....

2 kettling of demonstrators ....

3 transportation vessel ....

4 pillory ....

5 electronic tagging for offenders ....

2 What do you know about each image?

....

....

3 Do you think the following statements are true or false? Why? Now listen and check.

1 Homeless children were treated well in the 18th century.

2 In the past, women and men received different punishments.

3 William Wilberforce was a politician promoting civil rights.

4 Petty criminals were sent abroad in the 20th century.

B Modern civil rights movements in Britain

Listen and answer the following questions.

1 Which groups have been protected by recent British laws?

2 What was the result of the July 2005 bombings in London?

3 What are the most recent controversies?

4 What do some people feel about the European Parliament?

5 How important do you consider recent changes to British law? Why do you think this?

Discuss the following questions in your groups.

- What do you consider the most important developments in national and international law in the last twenty years? Why do you think this?

- How similar are the concerns of British people, about recent developments in law and policing, to your own concerns?

- In what ways have people's lives benefited from changes in the laws?

- What are the problems around law making? Why do you hold this view?

- What ways would you suggest to improve legal processes and policing for all countries?

a

b

c

d

e

17.1

The countryside and the seasons

TYPE OF ACTIVITY
Listening for information

LEVEL
Elementary to Pre-intermediate

TIME
40–50 minutes

AIMS
To find out about wildlife, the four seasons and the climate in Britain

VOCABULARY
autumn, blossom, grow, season, spring, summer, wildlife, winter

PREPARATION
One photocopy of the worksheet for each learner. Display pictures of animals found in the UK. A set of dictionaries.

Warmer

Ask learners what wild animals there are in the UK and to name any plants. Prompt with *trees, flowers, fruit and vegetables, wild and garden plants*. Write their answers on the board. Alternatively, learners work in groups of two or three and write down the names of as many UK animals and birds, or fruit and vegetables as possible in two minutes. Go over their answers as a group. Write the four seasons on the board and ask learners if they can name them. Ask what the temperatures are at this time of year in the UK.

A ▶ 70 Give one copy of the worksheet to each learner. Focus on exercise 1. Learners work in pairs and identify vocabulary on the picture (they can use dictionaries). Go over answers with the class. Tell learners that they're going to listen to a man talking about the countryside. Learners listen and tick the plants or animals she talks about. Go over answers with the class.

> **Answers**
> squirrel, deer, rabbit, eagle, fox

B ▶ 71–74 Learners work in pairs, writing the names of the seasons on the pictures. Check their answers. Play the second part of the audio, a short description of each season. Learners identify which season each person talks about and check answers in pairs. They listen again to complete the information gaps. Go over answers with class.

> **Answers**
> 1 autumn: 1st day 21st Sept; weather: windy and quite wet; average temperature: 9 degrees
> 2 summer: 1st day 21st June; weather: can rain but also very warm; average temperature: 20–28 degrees
> 3 winter: 1st day 21st December; weather: very cold, snowy and icy; average temperature: 4 degrees
> 4 spring: 1st day 21st March; weather: mild – sunny or rain; average temperature: 10–15 degrees

Point out that people use both Celsius and Fahrenheit (especially older people) and that it's usually colder in Scotland and the north of England, wetter in the west and often warmer in the south/south east of Britain.

C Tell learners that British people talk about the weather a lot, often when they are just meeting briefly in the street, or with someone they don't know well, to pass the time or break the ice. Focus on the useful expressions about the weather. Learners work in pairs and complete the expressions. Go over the answers with the class. Learners could then practise these as conversation openers as a role play.

> **Answers**
> 1 weather   2 hot   3 June   4 day   5 longer   6 warmer

Extension

The warmer can be used to highlight some spelling patterns: same spelling for some single and plural nouns (*sheep, deer, salmon, trout*); *-y/-ies* (*pony/ponies*); irregular patterns (*goose/geese, mouse/mice*). Learners can research more about British weather on www.woodlands-junior.kent.sch.uk (an excellent school site with an appropriate level of English). Learners discuss and compare the weather in their countries in small groups; highlight the use of the adverb as in the question *What's the weather like in your country?* Check the common response error, *It's like …*

A In the countryside

1 Match each picture to a word in the box.

eagle
deer
field
fox
oak tree
rabbit
river
squirrel
swan
wood

2 Listen to the man talking about the countryside where he lives in Scotland. Put a tick by the animals he talks about from the list.

B The seasons in the UK

Tell your partner what you can see in two of the pictures of the seasons. Then listen to the audio and write in the missing words.

1 ....
1st day:
Weather:
Average temperature:

2 ....
1st day:
Weather:
Average temperature:

3 ....
1st day:
Weather:
Average temperature:

4 ....
1st day:
Weather:
Average temperature:

C Talking about the weather

In the UK the weather changes a lot. Very often, people talk about the weather when they first meet. Read the sentences people often say. Write the correct words in the gaps.

day   hot   June   longer   warmer   weather

1 What nice .... we're having!

2 Ooh, isn't it .... today?

3 It's very wet for .... !

4 What a lovely .... !

5 The days are getting .... now!

6 It's .... than yesterday.

17.2

The town and the countryside

TYPE OF ACTIVITY
Listening and discussion

LEVEL
Intermediate

TIME
45–60 minutes

AIMS
To compare life in towns and the country in Britain

VOCABULARY
environment, fox/drag hunting, hunt, in the middle of nowhere, participate, point to point, race, way of life

PREPARATION
One photocopy of the worksheet for each learner. Intermediate level dictionaries. Option: more pictures of town and country life.

Warmer

Ask learners what they know about the British countryside. Tell them that in the UK many people go to the countryside at the weekends. Explain that, as the UK is comparatively small, people can easily access the countryside. Ask learners if they can name five activities they think British people like to do, or watch, in the countryside.

Tell learners they're going to find out more about typical town and country life. Learners look at the pictures on the worksheet and, in pairs/groups, divide these into activities usually found *in the countryside* and those usually found *in cities/towns*, or *either*. Option: extend this activity by displaying more pictures. Help with the vocabulary as necessary. Go over the answers as a class, checking and practising pronunciation.

Answers

Countryside activities
Village fete. Others: agricultural shows, archaeological sites, archery, drag hunting, hiking, horse riding/show jumping, shooting, medieval festivals, visiting National Trust buildings and gardens (palaces, castles, stately homes; note that some historic buildings are privately owned).

Town/city activities
Skateboarding. Others: aquarium, greyhound racing, major art galleries, bowling, cinema, ice skating, museums, pigeon racing, shopping, swimming, sports centre, theatre.

Either countryside or town activities
art exhibitions, barbecues, carnivals, cat/dog shows, cricket, dancing, football, golf, horse racing, tennis, local museums, private open gardens and houses, private parties, pubs, theme parks

---

▶ 75–78 Tell learners they are going to hear people talking about their way of life. Pre-teach any new vocabulary and focus on the topics *work, housing, way of life* and *environment*. Learners listen and take notes under the headings or allocate one column for each learner to complete. Play the audio twice for learners to complete their sections and check answers in pairs. Go over the answers as a class and discuss any points arising. Focus on the discussion activity and encourage them to exchange information. Alternatively, to develop the discussion more, learners complete short notes about their country using the same topic headings prior to their discussion.

Answers

	Countryside	City/Town
Work	more difficult to find; no job security	easier to get work; don't have to travel so far; better pay
Housing	high cost/scarcity of housing for renting and buying	cheaper flats and houses to rent; more choice
Way of life	relaxed, slower pace of life; everyone knows each other; sense of community; boring for young people	more fun; exciting, makes you feel good; more choice of activity
Environment	healthier than city; more space; grow your own vegetables	noisy day and night; crowded; polluted

---

Extension

Learners write a comparison of life in the British countryside and towns. This can also be useful as a collaborative writing activity with each learner writing one section, to be put together with visuals and displayed on the wall. Use the self-checking (error correction) box from *ESOL Activities Entry 3*, to encourage learner accuracy.

Listen to the audio about life in the town and countryside in the UK.

Write short notes on what the people say under the headings in the boxes below.

	Countryside	City/Town
Work		
Housing		
Way of life		
Environment		

Discuss the following questions in your groups.

- Compare the differences between the town and the city in Britain, using each heading as a guideline. Discuss these differences with a partner.
- In your country, what are the differences between life in the country and the towns and cities?
- What are the problems facing people who live in towns and cities? And in the countryside?
- What should we do to protect our different ways of living and our environment more?

UK country matters

TYPE OF ACTIVITY
Reading, gap fill and discussion

LEVEL
Advanced

TIME
45–60 minutes

AIMS
To gain an understanding of the concerns of rural Britain

VOCABULARY
blame, custodian, feature, hedgerow, iconic, intensify, plough, ramble, right to roam, rural

PREPARATION
One photocopy of the worksheet for each learner.
Option: display pictures of the British countryside and prepare a vocabulary and definition matching activity.

Warmer

Ask learners what they know about life in the British countryside and if they can name any areas of specific beauty, interesting sites, features or traditions of rural Britain. (This can be a review of earlier units.) Show some pictures of popular attractions from previous lessons, as prompts. Ask learners what they think *the values* are that the countryside represents to the British (*tradition, history, stability, cultural value, beauty*).

Attractions: the Cairngorm mountains, the Trossachs, the Western Isles (Scotland); the Antrim Plateau (Northern Ireland); the Brecon Beacons, Pembrokeshire coast, Snowdonia (Wales); Dartmoor, the Lake District, the New Forest, the Peak District, the Yorkshire Dales, Windsor Great Park (England)

Features: the Angel of the North, the Cerne Giant, Stonehenge, Wilmington Man

Traditions: deer/grouse/pheasant shooting, fishing, fox hunting (banned in 2000), golf, Morris dancing, steeple chasing, Sunday lunch in country pubs or at home, Christmas/Easter and other festivals or traditions, the Proms, charitable events, cricket, fishing, football, Glastonbury Festival, weekend walks in the countryside/seaside/gardens/stately homes

Tell learners they are going to explore issues in the UK countryside and some of the problems it faces. Give a copy of the worksheet to each learner. Focus on the title *UK Country matters*. Check that the learners understand its different meanings (as a verb: *to matter*, meaning the country(side) is important; as a noun: *a matter*, meaning country concerns or issues).

1   Learners read the text, underlining any new vocabulary and expressions. Option: use a vocabulary and definition matching activity, if prepared. In pairs, learners guess the correct vocabulary and list the main topics. They then complete the text and select the correct italic words to form collocations. As a discussion follow up, learners explore the values the land inspires within their own cultures.

> **Answers**
> 1   positive story
> 2   unique position
> 3   increasingly fragmented
> 4   tranquil fields
> 5   genetically modified
> 6   intensive food

Topics covered: strong relationship between British people and the land (right to roam); pressure on the farmers (to protect the countryside and be custodians of the land, i.e. not paid); problems for agriculture in general (low supermarket prices pushing prices down and forcing farmers out of business); imports contain genetically modified crops which are not allowed to be grown here (a strongly held opinion in the UK); people demand cheap food.

2   Check that learners understand the vocabulary, using dictionaries if necessary.

3   Learners prioritise the issues in the text, discuss the issues as a class and focus on the 'Problem-solving Tree'. Explain that it is used to explore problems and find solutions in a range of contexts. Explain that learners will be looking at issues related to the (UK) countryside, reflecting on these and considering solutions to environmental problems. Go through the worksheet instructions. Ask them what environmental concerns they have, from the text or from their own experience. Learners do the problem solving activity in pairs/groups and develop solutions together. Option: use the activity to make a 'why' tree, to work out solutions, either to environmental questions or others. Write down a problem and ask five questions with *Why?* to reach the core problem and find a solution.

Extension

Learners research different aspects of conflict between urban and rural environments online, both in Britain and across the world.

The relationship between the British and the countryside is essentially a very **1** .... *history/story*. With over 10,000 miles of public footpaths and 'right-to-roam' laws enabling walkers to wander through swathes of countryside, British people are in a **2** .... *position/place* to access green space. However, this relationship is in danger of becoming **3** .... *fragmented/fragile*. Farmers are often described as custodians of the land and required to keep fields unploughed as set-aside, pressured to maintain woodland and hedges and to enable ramblers to roam on footpaths and bridleways that criss-cross their land. They are also held responsible for keeping the identity of the landscape as essentially 'British' – a scene of **4** .... *fields/paths* dissected by flower-bedecked hedgerows – and all this is before they've even grown anything to eat!

In British agriculture there are huge economic conflicts. Firstly, there is pressure on farmers to intensify production. However, antipathy towards **5** .... *changed/modified* crops has led to Britain's ban on the growing of such food – but it is still present in imports. Supermarkets are blamed for pushing down the prices farmers are paid for their products, forcing small producers out of business – but British people keep buying low-cost food. If we keep demanding a pretty, rural environment free from massive cow sheds and other examples of **6** .... *food/animal* production but still expect cheap food, the question is – who will pay for it?

1 Read the text above. In pairs, complete the text with the words below and choose the correct alternative from the words in *italics*.

genetically   increasingly   intensive
positive   tranquil   unique

2 Explain the meaning of the following words and expressions.

antipathy   bridleway   flower-bedecked
massive   right-to-roam   swathes

3 List the key points that the author is making in the text. Which would you say is most important?

How to use the Problem-Solving Tree

- Draw a copy of the tree on to paper.

- Write the issue or context on the trunk of the tree (in this case the countryside, or the environment).

- Discuss key problems facing the countryside in Britain today. Write down one key problem on each root of the tree.

- Discuss solutions to each of these problems as a group.

- Write your solutions down around the apples in the branches.

- Use the branches to explain in detail how your solutions will work (by doing what?).

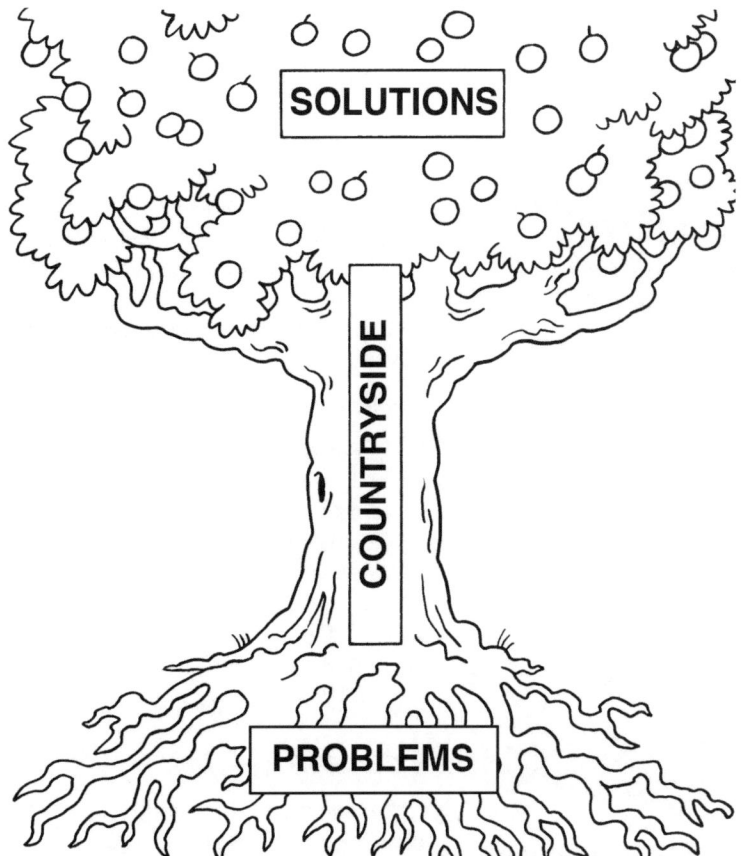

SOLUTIONS

COUNTRYSIDE

PROBLEMS

18.1

TYPE OF ACTIVITY
Reading and matching activity

LEVEL
Elementary to Pre-intermediate

TIME
40–50 minutes

AIMS
To find out about Britain's membership in organisations

VOCABULARY
currency, democracy, empire, government, include, keep the peace, member, permanent, sort out a problem, trade, Commonwealth, European Union, United Nations

PREPARATION
One set of cards for each pair/group of learners. Option: display flags of different international organisations and member countries and a map of the old British Empire. Outline map of the world, without country names.

Britain and the rest of the world

Warmer

On the board, write *the European Union*, *the United Nations* and *the Commonwealth* (started at the end of the British Empire) and the acronyms (EU, UN). Ask what they know about these organisations, e.g. *What groups of countries are members of them? Is Britain a member? What do they do? Why is this important?* Check their understanding of *empire* and elicit some other examples, e.g. Persia, Rome, Turkey (Ottoman), Russian, Spanish, French. Finally, display the flags of the organisations if available. Ask if they can match them.

Tell learners they're going to find out more about Britain in the world. Give a set of cards to each pair/group. They match the questions with the information, without reading in detail. (This is a good opportunity to show them how to scan for information.) Check these with the class. Learners then read the cards and answer questions together. Go over answers with the class.

Answers

	A	B	C	D
1	about 20% of the area of the world	six countries (Belgium, France, West Germany, Italy, Luxembourg and the Netherlands)	after the 2nd World War	1947
2	parts of Asia, Africa, the Americas and Australasia	1973	about 190	54
3	EU, the UN and the Commonwealth	They work in the EU parliaments and make new laws.	try to stop wars and to try to sort out problems in the world	to make government and democracy stronger and to end poverty

Write the names of the countries below on the board. Put their flags on the walls around the room for learners to match the countries and flags. Or place an outline map of the world (without country names) on the wall for learners to identify the countries on the map. Go over these with the class. Then learners walk around and guess which organisations they are members of (UN, Commonwealth or EU) and their relationship with the UK. Discuss any points arising with the class. This is a useful activity to show how widespread the old British Empire was and how it still impacts today through the Commonwealth to promote trade and good governance.

Organisations and countries

1 USA (UN, an ex-colony but never joined Commonwealth)
2 India (UN, Commonwealth, 'the Jewel of the Empire')
3 Jamaica (UN, Commonwealth)
4 South Africa (UN, Commonwealth)
5 Australia (UN, Commonwealth)
6 Guyana (UN, Commonwealth – the only South American country in the Commonwealth)
7 Rwanda (UN, joined the Commonwealth in 2009)
8 Germany (UN, EU).
  The UK is the only member country of all three organisations.

Extension

Use an old map to look at the extent of the old British Empire. Learners make a wall chart or a page for their British culture book/blog on the history of the Empire, the role of Europe and/or the UN, using information from websites. Learners can find out about Britain's role in these organisations (see *ESOL Activities Entry 3*, unit 15 for information on this). Teachers can find out about the history of migration online.

A

1 How big was the British Empire?

2 What places were in the British Empire?

3 Britain is a member of what organisations?

In the past Britain had a large empire and it covered about 20% of the world. From the 17th century, Britain controlled many areas of the world, in Asia, Africa, the Americas and Australasia. The Empire only lasted until the 20th century when most countries were independent again.

Now Britain is a member of important international groups such as the European Union, the United Nations and the Commonwealth.

B

1 Who started the European Union?

2 When did Britain join the EU?

3 What do MEPs do?

In 1957 six Western European countries joined together and started the European Economic Community. Britain joined in 1973 and there are now 27 member countries – it's now called the European Union. The EU has its own currency, the euro, but Britain still uses the pound.

Every five years there is a European election. Britain has 72 Members of the European Parliament (MEPs). They work in the EU parliaments in Strasbourg and Brussels, and make new laws for their countries.

C

1 When did the United Nations start?

2 How many countries are in the UN?

3 What does this organisation do?

Britain is also a member of the United Nations. There are about 190 countries in this organisation. The UN started after the Second World War to try to stop wars and solve the problems in the world. Britain is one of five full-time members of the United Nations Security Council. This council tries to keep peace between countries. The main office for the UN is in New York.

D

1 When did the Commonwealth start?

2 How many countries are there in the Commonwealth?

3 What does this organisation do?

The Commonwealth has 54 members – about a quarter of all the countries in the world.

Most of the countries were once part of the British Empire. The modern Commonwealth started in 1947, after many countries became free from British control. There is no leader but the Queen is the head of the Commonwealth. This organisation wants to make government and democracy stronger in countries and wants to end poverty.

18.2

TYPE OF ACTIVITY
Information exchange and listening

LEVEL
Intermediate

TIME
50–60 minutes

AIMS
To explore Britain's world role to present times

VOCABULARY
carbohydrates, death rate, diet, discovery, healthcare, invent, invention, life expectancy, obesity, process, shipping, trade

PREPARATION
Two sets of information cards for each group of four learners. One copy of question card and audio card (21st century Britain) for each learner. Intermediate dictionaries.

The journey to the 21st century

Warmer

Learners brainstorm important *discoveries* and *inventions* there have been and elicit the difference between the two terms. (*discovery*: finding something that already exists; *invention*: creating something new.) Ask them how these have benefited our lives and if they know any things that were discovered/invented by British people. Finally, they briefly compare life in Britain now, in the 21st century, to life a hundred years ago. Prompt with things like *work*, *diet* (food/drink) and *health*. Write down some of the key differences on the board.

Examples

Discoveries: electricity, gas, oil, steam power; medicines, e.g. antibiotics

Inventions: machinery/equipment, e.g. washing machine, gas/electric cookers, the telephone, car, train, bus, computer, Internet

Differences: change from agriculture to industry and technology, bigger population, longer life expectancy, cleaner water, better healthcare, NHS, better food, variety of work, better services, more education, pensions, shorter working week

Tell learners they are going to find out about some changes that happened in the UK in the 19th and 20th centuries. Learners work in groups of four. Give out sets of information cards to each pair, two with Card A and two with Card B. Give a copy of the question card C to each learner. Learners read through their information card and check the meaning of any new vocabulary with their partner (who has the same card, A or B). They then work out the questions to find the same information for the other century.

Suggested questions

What was the population in the *19th* century? What was the life expectancy? What work did people do at this time? How did people relax? What was British people's health/diet like at this time? What was the world news at this time?

Learners ask and answer each other's questions to exchange information. Go over the cards discussing and comparing the differences in people's lives.

▶ 79 Learners then listen to a talk about 21st century Britain. Give out the blank information cards. Learners complete the notes and check answers in pairs. Play the audio again and go over answers with the class. Discuss the information point by point. Compare facts from one century to the next and discuss the implications for us today, e.g. increase in life expectancy = more housing, food, healthcare, jobs needed, an ageing population takes up more healthcare resources.

Answers	
Population: approx. 61 million	**Diet**: unhealthy diet (too much fat and sugar), fresh food is becoming popular
Life expectancy: women 82, men 78	**Leisure**: television and film/DVDs and computer games are popular, also pubs and dancing
Work: NHS, tourism, local government, IT, banking, business, manufacturing, call centre/shop work	**World news**: the century started with wars in Afghanistan and Iraq, the UK supports international action to slow down climate change, politicians debate the future role of the UK in the world
Health: problems include heart disease, cancer, obesity, alcoholism and smoking	**Home news**: a huge crash in world markets affected economy, the gap between rich and poor widened

Extension

Groups put together the paragraphs to make a collaborative social history document. Encourage them to include photos, drawings or visuals and extra information from the Internet. This information can then be added to their British culture blog/book. They could also discuss in small groups what they think life will be like in Britain (or generally) a hundred years from now.

A 19th century Britain

Population: approximately 30 million in 1851

Life expectancy: the rich 50   the poor 20–35

Work: farming, factory work: in cotton, cloth, iron; trading and shipping; domestic work, clerks, shop workers

Leisure: fairs, racing, skating, parlour games

Health: poor health with very high birth rates, and also death rates due to disease: smallpox, typhoid, tuberculosis; terrible living conditions for the poor in industrial cities and towns

Diet: food from markets and street sellers; food staples were potatoes, bread; rich people ate a lot of meat, even children drank beer as it was often safer than water.

World news: 1805 Napoleon's fleet defeated by Nelson; 1833 slavery made illegal in Empire

Home news: 1800 the United Kingdom of Great Britain and Ireland was formed; 1829 the first modern police force was started; the Industrial Revolution progresses; 1837–1901 Queen Victoria reigned over the British Empire

B 20th century Britain

Population: approximately 50 million in 1951

Life expectancy: women 49   men 45 (1901)

Work: large manufacturing industries: ships, cars, building & heavy/light industry; offices and shops; agriculture and food production

Leisure: cinema, pubs, dancing; then after 1950s television, stereo music, CDs and computers in 90s

Health: better health with much lower child mortality rates; National Health Service set up; medical developments included penicillin, antibiotics, vaccines

Diet: mainly local food until the 1950s; arrival of first supermarkets, processed, tinned and imported food

World news: two world wars dominated first half of century; 1990 first Gulf war began; Britain was central in setting up United Nations, Commonwealth and later joined European Union

Home news: standard of living improved dramatically – gas, electricity, clean water in homes; 1918 women over 30 got the right to vote; 1921 partition of Ireland; the cost of houses increased greatly at the end of the century

C Journey to the 21st century

In groups of four, ask your partners about the following points:

- the population of Britain
- life expectancy of British people
- work people did at this time
- leisure time
- health in Britain
- British people's diet
- world news
- Britain's home news

.... century Britain

Population: ....

Life expectancy: Women .... Men ....

Work: ....

Health: ....

Diet: ....

Leisure: ....

World news: ....

Home news: ....

18.3

Values and visions

TYPE OF ACTIVITY
Reading and
information
exchange

LEVEL
Advanced

TIME
50–60 minutes

AIMS
To gain an
understanding of
Britain's values

VOCABULARY
advocate, colonial,
colony, divisive,
encapsulate,
international
relations, psyche,
reinvent, soul
search, strut, think
tank, transmute,
value, value base,
vision

PREPARATION
One photocopy of
the worksheet for
each pair, cut into A
and B cards. Take in
flip chart paper,
pens and advanced
dictionaries.

Warmer

Tell learners that they are going to explore British values and visions today. Ask learners what they understand by a country's *values*. Write their suggestions on the board. Then discuss what they understand by the *visions* a country may have for itself. Feed back.

> **Possible answers**
> **Values:** democracy, equal opportunities, equal rights, free trade, freedom of expression, human rights, independent legal system, open government, right to free choice, right to free education and healthcare, religious tolerance
> **Visions:** better healthcare, cleaner and healthier environment, full employment, greater equality, stronger role in international affairs, stronger economy

Option 1: split reading
Give out Part A to one pair of learners and Part B to another pair. They read their articles and check vocabulary, then note down the key points. They swap sections, read the new information and find out the meanings of new words from their partner. Together they find the answers to the questions on Cards A and B. Feed back.

Option 2: pairwork reading
Divide learners into A/B pairs. Give out one reading card to each learner but not the question cards. Ask learners to read through the information and underline important points. Learners explain what they have read to their partner and discuss what they found important. Give out the questions for Part A. Learners find the answers together. Then do the same with Part B. Go over the answers with the class.

> **Answers for Part A**
> **1** from being an ex-colonial power to having a more modest role in international relations **2** Britain joined the EU and has become a strong advocate for trade and development; Britain's military role has been questioned **3** how long will English be the dominant world language? **4** It has been described as 'a junior partner to the US' which British people find difficult.
>
> **Answers for Part B**
> **1** a possible breakup of the union (devolution); the shift of power away from Europe **2** its ability to react to change and reinvent itself **3** it hasn't got a written constitution, but it has the Magna Carta of 1215 (described as the most important constitutional document of all time) **4** a change in economic power, e.g. China, India, Brazil and possible loss of influence in financial markets

Ask what they find interesting or surprising in the text.

Extension

Discuss with learners the political and economic situations that are important at the time they are of working on this unit, both in the UK and throughout the world, or set up a discussion using questions such as *What values do you think are important for a country in the 21st century? What will worry people most in the 21st century? What visions are important for a country and its people? What strategies would you suggest to encourage world stability and peace?* Alternatively, learners can add a discussion site to their British culture blog/book.

Set up a semi-formal debate using ideas from the text, e.g. *This house believes that English will no longer be useful as the main International language in 75 years time*, or *The values of the past are no longer appropriate for the modern world*. Learners can take on different roles for the debate, e.g. Asian farmer, East African doctor, European single parent, South American miner, North American oil worker or manager, Chinese trade representative; business person, scientist, artist, historian, environmentalist.

A   Britain's changing world role

In recent decades the United Kingdom has had to take a long look at its changing role on the world stage. The last half century saw Britain transmute from an ex-colonial power with a recently dissolved Empire to a player with a more modest role in international relations. As its power base shrank, Britain had to re-invent itself, its values and its visions for the future, in a world of uncertainty and change. But this begs the question, what are the values and visions of the UK in the 21st Century?

A look at recent history denotes the changing role of the UK and also identifies a different value base emerging. Having survived two devastating European wars, a less isolated Britain has become a member state in the post-war European Union and a strong advocate for trade and development within its borders. Also, following two divisive wars in Iraq and Afghanistan, British people have questioned its military role and some difficult soul searching has taken place. A recent poll suggested that people were less convinced than ever of Britain's world role and a respondent likened it to, 'strutting around the world like a policeman'.

Controversially, a Conservative Prime Minister, David Cameron, defined the role of the UK as more a 'junior partner', in relationship to America, a view which does not sit comfortably within the British psyche. But in fact it is argued that this best describes the reality on the ground.

One certainty for Britain is that English is still the dominant world language of international commerce and communication and will remain so at present – but the real question is, for how long?

B   21st century values

In redefining the four nations' roles, there are many contradictions, still seemingly unresolved, that obscure a real vision for a 'British' future – and these cracks can appear to widen at any moment. For example, the desire in Scotland and in parts of Wales for greater nationhood or even independence could break up the Union. If these nations voted for separation from England, no one can truly estimate what the impact might be.

Taking a global view, the shift of power away from Europe continues. Although in 2010 the United Kingdom had the sixth largest GNP in the world, this power base could easily be swept away. With the rise of new economic powers such as China, India and Brazil, the United Kingdom's role is challenged. Just as the 60s saw the decline of the British steel industry and its allied trades, so the 21st century could see the decline of the British financial market and an end to its international role.

However, although the goalposts change, the UK's strength has always been its ability to react to change and reinvent itself, from a seafaring and trading nation to a manufacturer and then to a key financial player within international markets. 21st century think tanks analysing future trends may well find new routes for Britain to follow, to hold its position in the face of rapid technological development, environmental concerns and a shifting political map.

Britain has had no written constitution to define itself and encapsulate its values and visions since the Magna Carta of 1215. Perhaps however this offers the nation greater opportunity for reflection, re-evaluation and change.

Questions on Part B

1 What potential problems are facing modern Britain?

2 What has been a particular strength of Britain?

3 What is unusual about Britain's constitution?

4 What challenges must Britain respond to in the 21st century?

5 What future role would you foresee for Britain?

Questions on Part A

1 How has Britain's global position changed over the last century?

2 What are the values that have recently emerged in Britain?

3 What linguistic question does the writer raise?

4 What's problematic about Britain's relationship with the US?

5 What's your opinion of Britain's present world role?

Audioscript

1.1

▶ 2

England is the biggest country in the UK and over fifty million people live here. One famous place is the London Eye, a big wheel by the river Thames, in London. England is famous for its buildings, cricket and the writer, Shakespeare. The symbol of England is the rose.

▶ 3

Scotland has a population of over five million. A famous place is Ben Nevis, the highest mountain in Britain. Scotland is famous for whisky, the kilt that many men wear, and the Loch Ness monster! The symbol of Scotland is the thistle.

▶ 4

There are about two million people in Northern Ireland. A famous place you can see on the coast is the Giant's Causeway and there are many lovely villages in the countryside too. Northern Ireland's also famous for its traditional pubs, its music and dancing. One of the symbols of Northern Ireland is the shamrock.

▶ 5

Wales is very beautiful. About three million people live here. One famous place is Conwy castle, which you can see in the photo. It's also famous for its mountains, singing and rugby. One of the symbols of Wales is the leek.

▶ 6

England | Scotland | Northern Ireland | Wales

▶ 7

English | Scottish | Northern Irish | Welsh

1.3

▶ 8

When you're travelling in the UK, it's not difficult to see the attraction of living and working there. For me, the UK's a banquet, a feast of delights to make your mouth water! It's hard to believe that such a small place has so much to offer; take, for example, the snow-capped mountains of Wales and the Highlands of Scotland, or the azure waters of luscious Cornwall in the Southwest of England, with its sandy, surfing beaches. All over Britain, you can spend your days visiting ancient towns and villages and sit in pubs chatting to the locals, who are usually really friendly to you, wherever you're from.

Agreed, the UK is relatively expensive, but the combination of stunning scenery, amazing variety and compact geography is a unique draw. And then there's the island's extraordinary history … You can follow the Roman's footsteps on Hadrian's Wall between Scotland and England and visit the Braveheart battlefields or just go mystic at Stonehenge, stopping off at the Glastonbury festival en route. Then in Wales you can recall the legends of King Arthur as you hike up Mount Snowdon, and then head off to Northern Ireland for the Antrim Plateau and the stunning coastline.

And if all this gets too much, you can shift the pace up a gear, and experience Britain's world-class cities. Here you'll find great music, clubs and food and a thriving art scene.

Really, aged 17 or 70, the UK is yours for the taking, and it's all in a country which takes just 12 hours to drive through end to end!

▶ 9

What I've found on my journey around Britain has made me want out speak out, loudly and urgently. What I've discovered to my horror, is that that the Britain that-used-to-be, the four countries of quirkiness, history and difference and a people with a love of the land, and real, tangible region variation, you know, this is being systematically destroyed. Its individuality is being lost.

It's being shaped by the rise of culture missionaries, and by that I mean those people who are screaming for a, a smoke-free, well-dressed, designer nation whose values are those of big, faceless corporations and government. The final straw is our uniqueness and sense of humour, all being sort of blunted by a watering down of local distinctiveness and regional difference. And I believe all these factors have resulted in a 'cloning' effect on our society. And from our streets, our shopping centres, to our designer front rooms and kitchens, we've just become copies or clones of each other without any individuality left at all.

As for British people, I worry about how unaware most people are of this, you know, the bleaching out of our character, our community and sense of place, in fact, our entire identity as an island. And we seem to roll over to our new masters, you know, with no questioning, no imagination, and lazily consume a diet of soap operas, mass digital entertainment and tedious TV celebrity lives!

2.3

▶ 10

I think what people don't realise about our region is its historical importance and its variety, you know. Northumberland's the most northerly county in England, and what with everything so 'Londoncentric', the regions don't get a look in sometimes. But we've got World Heritage sites like Hadrian's wall, Lindisfarne Priory on Holy Island, then there's Bamburgh castle, home of the Northumberland Kings … and there are miles and miles of open, sandy beaches. Don't forget though, this region used to be important for shipping and there was ship building right up the rivers Tyne and Wear … but that's gone now. We're a friendly lot here though and we've got no pretences, like they have down south!

▶ 11

Now you see the Cotswolds stretches through the middle of England and, er, the hills run through several counties. And a lot of our villages start with the word Chipping, which means *market* in Old English. Erm, the wealth of this place came from sheep an' wool markets from the 1300s, well before tourism! Our village of course, Chipping Campden, is famous for Robert Dover's Olympic Games and Skuttlebrook Wake which started in 1612. Er, it's a bit drunken mind you, but it's all good fun. And then the Guild of Craftsmen came here in 1902 from East London, er, part of the Arts and Crafts movement. And now there are all them rock stars and politicians and the like, foreigners we call 'em, living here so we're a funny old mix really.

▶ 12

Well, the county of Derry's very old and in 1921 it became one of the six counties of Northern Ireland, er, part of the United Kingdom. Its main city has two names, Derry and Londonderry, which reflect its recent history but it has an ancient history too, going back to the 6th century and is actually the only completely walled city in the British Isles. Now it's shaking off its difficult past and it's a great place to visit … it's now a recognised centre for music and the arts and the UK City of Culture of 2013, which is all very exciting.

▶ 13

Well, I moved up here, to Ullapool, when we got married. I'm from Glasgow, see, but my wife er, she's a Highlander from north west Scotland. I love the people and the way of life here but the future's a bit uncertain at the moment, see … I'm a fisherman and that's a tough job with the EU quotas and all. But if we do move, we'll miss Ross and Cromarty so much. We thought of moving to Edinburgh, Aberdeen or back to Glasgow for my wife to get work as a teacher but moving back to the lowlands would be difficult as I'd miss the lochs and glens and the wee islands, you know, and you cannae beat the Highlands for romance!

▶ 14

I live on the Pembrokeshire coast, in the far South West of Wales, see. It's a spectacular area with wonderful seas and wildlife … eh, there's dolphins an' whales an 'puffins too, yes, plenty of them. Well, actually, my village St David's, isn't a village at all, er, it's the smallest city in Britain, and an ancient site of pilgrimage, the final resting place of our country's patron saint … and of course we've got our own language, *Ydych chi'n gallu siarad Cymraeg?*, which means 'Can you speak Welsh?'.

▶ 15

When I was a child I lived in the countryside in Kent, in the Southeast, the Garden of England … that's what they used to call it … and it was really a lovely time of my life. In the spring there was lambing and apple blossom in the orchards, it was just like paradise. Well, I'm 82 now and I've been living in the cathedral city of Canterbury for 40 years … and it's very nice here too, very quiet.

▶ 16

Our city Liverpool's amazing, and we were the City of Culture, like, a few years ago. 'Cos of the waterfront we're a World Heritage site too. And we had the Beatles and we got our two big footie teams, Liverpool and Everton, so we're really famous us Scousers actually! A lot of people can't understand folks from Merseyside 'cos of our accent like, so I hope you get what I'm saying … seeya love!

3.1
▶ 17

I'm a teacher in a big city in Northern Ireland with two names. It's called Londonderry and Derry. In the past there were problems between people who wanted to be British and people who wanted to be Irish but it's better now. I just say I'm Northern Irish!

▶ 18

I live with my mum and dad in Birmingham, in England. My mum's from Yorkshire. She's very funny and has a different accent to me. We often visit my mum's family in Leeds. My grandparents were born in Jamaica, in the Caribbean, and came here to work. My dad says he's British but my Mum says she's English. I say I'm black British.

3.2
▶ 19

In 1837 Queen Victoria was crowned and from this time there were many changes. In 1880, for example, education became compulsory for children up to ten. Also any man with land valued at £10 could now vote but that only added up to 24% of the population. In 1892, Mr Dadabhai Naoroji was the first Asian man to become a British MP but it was not until 1919 that the first woman took her seat as an MP and she was an American, Lady Astor. But the first woman who was actually elected as an MP was Constance Markiewicz in 1918 when she was in prison in London. She didn't take her seat as a protest, along with other Irish MPs.

Emmeline Pankhurst was one of many suffragettes who fought for votes for women. She was imprisoned with many others for protesting and demonstrating. One young woman, Emily Davison, was killed by the King's horse, when she ran under it at a race track in 1913. Women over 30 were finally given the vote in 1918, after the First World War. In the same year, school was made compulsory for all boys and girls up to the age of 14.

Moving on some years, it was again a war that changed the lives of many people. In the Second World War, women had to take over a lot of work usually done by men, like farming and construction. Interestingly, the new Waterloo Bridge in London was built mostly by women in 1942. Many young men lost their lives fighting and the average age of an air force fighter pilot at this time was only 20.

In the 60s many women demanded equal rights at work and equal pay. They were called feminists. All main jobs in Government usually went to men from public school. Eton for example, has produced 20 Prime Ministers, including David Cameron. In 1979 the first female Prime Minister, Mrs. Thatcher, was elected. She was called the 'Iron Lady' because she was a strong leader. Around this time, men's groups became a way for men to discuss problems such as their roles as fathers. Also, men fought for more legal rights to see their children if their marriages ended. Equal opportunities became stronger for all and Diane Abbott became the first black British woman MP in 1987. In 1990 Justin Fashanu became the first openly gay male footballer. In 1997, Prime Minister Tony Blair gave more jobs to women in the new Labour government but they were still called 'Blair's babes' by the press.

Nowadays men and women are much more equal. However, they still earn less than men. It also shows that only a third of men do housework even if both partners are working full time.

3.3

▶ 20

Interviewer: Where were you both born, Mr and Mrs Clarke?

Mary: Well, I was born in Camberwell in London, but Delroy was born in Jamaica and was 15 when he came to England.

Delroy: And we're in our 50s now, been married for 25 years and have a son and a daughter.

Interviewer: What work do you do?

Mary: Well, I work as a teacher trainer at university and Delroy's a self employed builder now but he was a graphic designer, and my daughter's an interpreter. And my son works for BT.

Interviewer: How would you describe your identity?

Delroy: What would you say? Um, I always tick the Black British box but the kids describe themselves as Black British Caribbean, but there isn't a box for that.

Mary: Yeah, I don't' think of myself as English but I suppose if I had to describe my identity it would be as a Londoner, yeah, Londoner. But also, another part of our identity is, er, we're regular church members, and that's a big part of our lives and defines our values and identity too really …

▶ 21

Interviewer: When did you come to the UK Sushil?

Sushil: I came over here when my wife died, in 1970. I got a work permit in India to work as an ESOL teacher and I came over with my son, who was just 5 then. I started teaching in London to women who really needed the language, you know, new migrants, and helped set up a Hindu temple. I'm 80 now.

Interviewer: What about you Raj?

Raj: Well, as dad said, I was a kid when I go here an' I'm 45 now, so I don't remember much about India. I've travelled around a bit, lived in Scotland and before that in New York. My ex-partner was Scots, and er, I moved back south a few years ago. Um, I'm in IT, freelance, and a single parent, and a carer!

Interviewer: How would you describe your identity?

Raj: As British Asian I suppose, well, yeah and Hindu, an' a strict vegetarian …

Interviewer: And what about you, Elisha?

Elisha: I'm 10 and I'm Scottish.

Raj: Yeah, but you've been in England for 7 years.

Elisha: Yeah but I'm still Scottish … and Indian.

Raj: Oh, ok.

Interviewer: What do you think of yourself as, Mr Sharma?

Sushil: Well, I call myself British - that's what's on my passport.

▶ 22

Interviewer: Can I ask a few personal details about your background, like where were you both born, your age, what you do?

Reza: OK. Actually, I'm Reza, I'm from Iran, I'm 30 and er, originally I was a refugee but I graduated in business college, and now work for a local company.

Ellie: Hi, I'm Ellie and I'm from Poland, I'm 37, and I came as a migrant worker 7 years ago, and got a job as an assistant manager in a care home for the disabled.

Interviewer: What religion are you?

Reza: Well, I'm a Muslim and Ellie's a Catholic. But neither of us is so strict, really …

Ellie: Yeah, we've been together for 6 years now and living together for about 4 … and we're getting married soon as we're going to have a family!

Interviewer: What do you see as your national identity?

Reza: Well, I'm still Iranian but I have a British passport. But as for my identity, actually I'm Azari, from a small region in Iran.

Ellie: And, I'm still Polish but I have the right to live and work here under the EU law.

4.3

▶ 23

Edward Miliband (Leader of the Opposition): Mr Speaker, can the Prime Minister tell us, how is his 'big society' going?

David Cameron (The Prime Minister): I believe … I believe … I actually believe that almost every single Member of this House of Commons actually backs what we're talking about. Let me just explain what it is. The idea of devolving power to local authorities, and beyond to communities, that was in his manifesto, it was in my manifesto, it was indeed in the Liberal Democrat manifesto. I think we all support it. The idea of opening up public services to more local involvement and control, again, it was in all of our manifestos, and we support it. And I believe that probably every single Member of the House spends time in their own constituency encouraging volunteering, encouraging philanthropic giving, and wanting people to play a bigger part in a bigger society. I think the whole House is united over it.

Speaker: Mr. Miliband.

Edward Miliband: Mr Speaker, Mr Speaker, we all support thriving communities, and that's why there is such concern from charities up and down the country. Now why doesn't he listen to people who know a lot about volunteering, like Dame Elisabeth Hoodless, the Chief Executive of the Community Service Volunteers, the largest volunteering charity in Britain? She says the Prime Minister's policies are 'destroying the volunteer army'.

David Cameron: Obviously, I don't agree with what she has said, but I want to work with all those involved in charities and voluntary bodies to encourage them to play a strong part in this. And we are putting £470 million across this spending review into charities and voluntary bodies. We are also establishing a £100 million transition fund to help charities affected by cuts. And something I can tell him for the first time today, because of our deal with the banks, the big society bank - wait for it, wait for it - the big society bank will be taking £200 million from Britain's banks to put into the voluntary sector. Labour would have got nothing out of the banks, so I am sure that he will want to stand up and welcome that.

Edward Miliband: Mr Speaker, Mr Speaker, he doesn't mention … he doesn't mention that he is cutting billions of pounds from voluntary sector organisations up and down this country. Now let's take an example … let's take an example of where parents volunteer in a crucial part of local communities: Sure Start. Before the election, he promised to protect Sure Start. In fact he decided to cut funding by 9%, and the Daycare Trust say 250 Sure Starts are expected to close. Can he tell us how's that helping the big society?

5.1
▶ 24

The British Royal family's surname is Windsor. The Queen lives at Buckingham Palace in London and other family members live nearby. They go to Balmoral, a castle in Scotland, every year on holiday.

The king or queen is the Head of State. They have no real power but are still important. He or she opens Parliament, meets with presidents and heads of state, and visits different countries. The Prime Minister and the Government make new laws. Every week the Prime Minister goes to see the king or queen at Buckingham Palace to talk about the work that the Government is doing.

In the past, kings and queen had a lot of power and had very different lives. Some fought and died in battle at home and abroad. Others, like King Charles I, were executed. King Egbert was the first 'King of All England' in the 9th century. A tough English King called Edward I took control of Wales in 1282. The crowns of Scotland and England joined together in 1603, after Elizabeth I died - she had no children so James VI of Scotland, the son of Mary, Queen of Scots, was crowned James I of England, Scotland, Ireland and Wales. The oldest son of the king or queen is called the Prince of Wales but there is no Welsh king now. There have been over 200 kings and queens altogether.

5.3
▶ 25

Host: Good evening everyone and welcome to the Brighton Festival Debate. We're here tonight to discuss 'What divides Britain?'. A discussion on social construction and identity'. Now I'd like to put my first question to the author and scholar Evelyn Pickard. Evelyn, I believe you've just written a book, er, *Britain through the Looking Glass* …

Evelyn: Yeah, good evening Jeremy, it's about identity and the individual in Britain today.

Host: So would you like to start us off please with an overview of what, in your opinion, is *identity*?

Evelyn: Well, we can look at our identities, that is, who we are and how we see ourselves, in several different ways. So, people can see themselves in terms of, erm, wealth, poverty, er, gender, ethnicity and so on. But still, very important in Britain is social class or the class system - upper, middle and working class …

Host: So what do you think are the key factors that make British people see themselves as *different* from each other?

Evelyn: Well, we have these multiple identities, pulling us in different ways, and being a working mother too in Britain, don't I know it! But, interestingly enough, the class system is a sticking point in Britain … you know, I've studied class and it's still very much *alive* but often people don't want to talk about, or even acknowledge it exists. People are often still judged on their accent, their class accent.

Sophie: I don't quite agree with Evelyn there …

Host: Sophie, I should say, is an editor who comes from the upper end of the class system, would you agree?

Sophie: As do *you*, Jeremy … but I would also say we've got the so-called North-South divide, and regional accents … and we've also got a *southern* divide too where the difference in one's accent tells us where we've been educated for instance, as well as class. Um, compare, for example, the English that I was expected to produce when I was at private school, uh, called RP …

Ollie: The 'Queen's English'!?

Sophie: Yes, Ollie, if you like …

Evelyn: Can I just say that RP, or Received Pronunciation, sometimes called BBC English, isn't really a *standard* English spoken by most people, it's more that the southern English accent still has prestige, and reflects more middle class values and aspirations, er, and research suggests that RP is actually only spoken by 2% of the population …

Sophie: But as I was about to say, now, on balance, we're much more equal than we used to be and there's plenty of room for other types of spoken English. For instance, one can hear regional accents on the television. I mean, of course, there's a long way to go but there's *much more* equality than before, in a relatively class-free Britain … I think social class isn't the thing that opens or shuts doors now. Maybe it's a bit more about your *ability* and *drive* …

Host: Ollie, you come from a working-class background and you're a successful TV presenter… What do you make of this?

Ollie: Yeah, that's all very well Sophie, but you need to be a bit more cautious when you say these things, 'cos, we all agree out loud that class division is very outdated, and, we know it's wrong to judge someone by their accent, and to make assumptions about their background, abilities and so on - but it still happens, especially outside the media world. I think class still basically relates to a history of poverty and inequality of opportunity, and to prejudice, in a society where there's a lot of judgements made about people's class an' social status. Look, we *still* haven't got to the stage yet when the weather lady's saying 'it ain't gonna' rain today love', or someone with an accent like David Beckham is sitting there reading the six o'clock news … and I think it will be a long time before we do!

6.1
▶ 26

I like eating at pubs, like the Anchor Inn, it's my local, you know. You can have their steak and ale pies or ploughman's lunches, with cheese and chutney and homemade desserts afterwards.

🔘 **27**

I like going to tea shops, myself. My favourite is called the 18th Century Tea Rooms. I love their cream teas in summer and in winter I like having its hot teacakes, or crumpets, with butter, mmm … yummy.

🔘 **28**

I like fish and chips with lots of beans and onion rings. I don't like mushy peas though! Sometimes my dad and I go to the chippy on the corner, the chip shop, that is. It's called Bob's Cafe and it's really nice.

🔘 **29**

Well, my favourite restaurant is Tall Trees in the next town. You can eat our really good local Welsh lamb or try Scottish salmon. It's very good and not too expensive, and the puddings are wonderful.

🔘 **30**

Well, the All Day Breakfast is always popular but it's very filling. Usually you have eggs, bacon, sausage, mushrooms and beans and this can be with tomatoes or fried potatoes. You also get brown or white toast with butter and marmalade and this is served with tea or coffee and orange juice. It's great!

🔘 **31**

OK, most Ploughman's Lunches come with a white or brown roll or fresh bread, a piece of cheese – often local cheese – tomato, a pickled onion, an apple, some lettuce, some cucumber and chutney.

🔘 **32**

When you make a sherry trifle you need some sponge cakes, some apricot or raspberry jam, some vanilla custard and double cream, some almonds, and you can use sweet sherry or liqueur if you want, and fresh fruit.

6.2

🔘 **33**

Presenter: Good morning Tom. Now, firstly, why has Britain had a reputation for poor food?

Expert: Good morning Paul. Well, for a long time it was very bad! Um, it probably started in the Industrial Revolution, when people moved from the countryside to the cities and often lived on poor quality meat and vegetables. So food was boiled down into thin stews to prevent disease and to the hide the taste of unpleasant, old ingredients. Then in the Second World War, the UK couldn't import food and so food rationing started. People just got used to a bland, tasteless diet.

Presenter: Do you think it's better now?

Expert: Definitely but it wasn't until the 1960s and 70s that things really changed and exciting imports of continental foods arrived in greengrocers and local markets began to sell all kinds of new vegetables, such as aubergines, green peppers, chillies … and continental herbs and spices arrived, and vegetarian food became popular too. You see, immigrants from all over the world arrived, bringing their food with them… Caribbean, European, Middle Eastern and Asian people. Today Indian food's the most popular takeaway in Britain, with over 8,000 Indian restaurants and some curry dishes even originate here. What could be more British than going for a curry on a Friday night?

Presenter: Well, that's true. So the international influence has been positive?

Expert: Absolutely. But in recent years, people have also begun to appreciate their local foods more too.

Presenter: What do you think are the regional food highlights within the UK?

Expert: Wow, so many. Regional dishes abound here but they're usually quite simple and hearty and often with an interesting history. For example, er, Cornish pasties from the West Country were first made for the tin miners and one half of the filling was meat, and the other half fruit. And then another favourite is the cream tea, that's scones eaten with clotted cream and jam and a cup of tea. And in Scotland, there's haggis and venison, Scotch broth and Cock-a-leekie soup. From the north of England you've got Cumberland sausage and Lancashire hotpot, er, a stew, and black pudding, which is a kind of sausage made from pig's blood. There's pie and mash in London, where, in fact, fish and chips were first sold together as a meal over a hundred years ago.

Presenter: What about Wales and Northern Ireland?

Expert: OK, there's Welsh cheeses, which are really quite unique and delicious too, and laverbread, or to give it its Welsh name, Bara lawr. That's a real speciality made of seaweed and oats, really good … And from Northern Ireland there's Dulse, which is fried seaweed, and Fadge, a potato bread, and some excellent seafood. And many regions across Britain produce fantastic cheeses, jams, chutneys, honey, local pies or sausages and meat. Go to any farmers' market and you'll see.

Presenter: And what about dessert?

Expert: Well, you know there are literally hundreds of different kinds of British puddings, from sherry trifles and fruit crumbles to the funnily-named Spotted Dick … as well as er, tarts and crumbles, which have become very popular again even with gourmet chefs. And finally a recent favourite to arrive on the scene is Banoffee pie, made from a banana and toffee mix on a biscuit base with strawberries and double cream … mm … delicious!

Presenter: Mm … mouth watering … and what about drinks?

Expert: OK, as for drinks, there's always been great beer, and whisky from Scotland, and Ireland too … but Britain also has over 300 vineyards and produces much of its own wine for export.

7.1

🔘 **34**

thirty 'p' | ninety nine 'p' | one pound fifty | two pounds fifteen | thirty five pounds and seven 'p' | a tenner | twelve ninety-nine | a quid

9.2

▶ 35

Welsh legend says that fairies live on the hill where, in 1833, in the village of Mold, farmers found a stone grave with a skeleton of a teenage boy or girl, buried with a beautiful gold cape and jewellery. It's thought to be over 3,000 years old and was probably the grave of a person of great importance. The delicate cape was made from one piece of beaten gold. It shows how, even at this time, advanced communities travelled and shared their knowledge in Europe.

▶ 36

One of the most important finds in Britain was the ancient Sutton Hoo ship grave in Suffolk, England. It shows us amazing 7th century technology years after the Romans left Britain. This great buried ship, similar to those found in Scandinavia, contained valuable goods: armour, furs, and delicate gold jewellery from Anglo-Saxon Britain. It was found in 1939, the year the Second World War began, and the magnificent, bronze helmet became a symbol of survival.

▶ 37

In 1831, on the Isle of Lewis, 78 12th century chess pieces were found. They were made from walrus ivory and whales' teeth. Chess, a game of war between royalty, knights and priests, came from India and through the Middle East around 500BC to reach this tiny Scottish island via Scandinavia. This find reminds us of the connection between North Europe and Britain.

▶ 38

High Cross can be found at Ardboe, in Northern Ireland. Now a national monument, it was the first high cross built in Ulster. Dating from the 8th or 9th century, it measures 5.5 metres high and 1 metre wide. Its 22 carved panels show Biblical scenes. There are also the remains of an abbey here, founded by Saint Coleman in 590 AD. It reminds us of the impact of the arrival of St Patrick in Ireland.

9.3

▶ 39

Fleming was born to a Scottish sheep-farming family in 1881 and became a doctor in 1906. He discovered penicillin by accident when he noticed what happened to mould in a laboratory dish he'd left open. It was a discovery that would change history. An active ingredient in mould, which he named penicillin, turned out to be the most powerful life-saving drug in the world at the time and would alter forever the treatment of bacterial infections.

This work gave rise to a huge pharmaceutical industry, producing synthetic penicillin that would conquer some of mankind's most ancient afflictions, including syphilis, gangrene and tuberculosis. I think he's saved more lives than any other Briton.

▶ 40

Known as 'Mother Seacole' by the soldiers of the Crimean War, Mary Seacole was a devoted nurse. Born in Kingston, Jamaica in 1805, to a Scottish soldier and a Jamaican mother, Mary funded her own journey to the Crimea and treated the severely wounded, using traditional remedies from Jamaica.

She returned from the battlefields to England, almost penniless. But a fund was set up by friends, and a benefit concert attended by thousands of people, was held by the military in London, to raise money to support her. She also joined the periphery of the royal circle and used to treat the Prince of Wales's medical problems. She later wrote a book about her life and travels and was voted first place in an online poll of 100 Great Black Britons.

10.3

▶ 41

A: Well, I think the welfare state supports a huge range of our needs, all our health care requirements and psychiatric support, and there's family and children's' support through social services. As well as looking after people who are out of work. What more can you ask for?

B: Hang on though, it's not perfect. We sometimes wait longer in the NHS for operations, and the fact is, the quality of care's suffering because of pressure of beds and overworked health staff. And anyway it doesn't include everything – what about dental treatment and glasses?

C: The biggest problem is that it all costs the taxpayer far too much money. We need to come up with a better welfare system too, something that'll take the lazy people out of dependency on welfare and get them back into work!

A: I don't know why you're so negative. The benefits system just offers help to people who need it, you know, incapacity benefit for those too ill or disabled to work, people who aren't as lucky as you, those who really need help. What can they do if they're out of work and have families to feed, and what about support for people on low incomes?

B: I agree in theory, but it's unsustainable. The country's in debt – how are we supposed to pay for it all?

A: From our taxes, of course, and we should tax the rich and big businesses more. You know, we've got an amazing system compared to what they had in the past, and we need to protect it. Yes, it's expensive, but at least people have their basic needs covered and aren't left out on the streets …

C: So why should the rich pay for everyone else?

A: To make a fairer society. It's obvious that a more equal society is a happier one.

C: That's idealistic nonsense. Public services are expensive and totally inefficient. And what about the independence of the individual?

A: Well, what about the individual's responsibility to society? I reckon you'd rather have two societies: one for the rich and another for the poor.

B: OK, OK … but let's focus on the practical issues: the elderly, for example. We're not getting any younger and by 2020 half our population's going to be over sixty, and there'll be no one working to pay for it all! It'll all just be too expensive! We've got to take action now to cut back …

A: Well people will be working for longer and there's plenty of pension schemes to support people in retirement. Other countries manage so why can't we?

11.1

▶ 42

Older people go to out to the pub more, er, on a Sunday for lunch, and a drink. Em, well I like having Sunday lunch in the pub with my family. But I like going out with my mates on a Friday or Saturday night, too. We usually go to our local pub, the Crown, and have a laugh.

▶ 43

Well, I think film's very popular here yeah, there's some great films around and good telly too ... but *really* I like going to the theatre, you know, er, it's different, its *real*, you know, er, and interesting.

▶ 44

Well, I used to do a lot of sport when I was young, I was quite good actually. Er, football was my game and then I became a referee. And now, I'm an armchair sportsman! Yes, I just watch it on the telly!

▶ 45

Woman: Umm, well we both like to get out and that sort of thing.

Man: Don't stay in much ... like to get out in the fresh air really ...

Woman: Yeah, and I think having a garden is just wonderful, ah, I really love my garden ...

Man: ... But I do the hard work, you see, and she just does the sitting!

▶ 46

OK, ... em, you know, you can go to a club any time really it's not that exciting so, I suppose, my favourite thing to do is um, well, go out to a concert and see er a band, you know, see some live music, it's cool, you know ...

11.3

▶ 47

Well, we've been there twice now and it just poured down the first time, oh man it was crazy! We were prepared like for rain 'cos summer festivals in Britain like WOMAD have got this reputation, but this was mad. The second time I went with my college mates, you know, and the music and the atmosphere were cool, yeah, we had a real laugh. The music's from all over the world and we saw some great bands from Senegal and Mali, from all over the place.

▶ 48

Em, as the name of this festival suggests, it's all about the famous ship the Titanic which was built here in Belfast. This is a week-long celebration held in April and it includes a whole range of events for all the family like exhibitions, tours, and film screenings about the building of the Titanic and its tragic maiden voyage. I suppose if you don't like boats and ships maybe this festival's not for you, but most people have a fabulous week.

▶ 49

Everyone usually loves the Highland Games because it's so quirky and unique to Scotland. I mean, strange sports like tossing the caber, you know, a huge tree trunk and, and the Scottish hammer throw as well as bagpipe playing and country dancing. Highland Games go on throughout the year actually, but the most famous event is the Cowal Highland Gathering. But, uh, you've got to watch out for the midges – they'll bite you to death if they can.

▶ 50

I've been coming to Hay-on-Wye since it began in 87, and if you like books, literature and debate, and the performing arts too, then this festival's for you. The Hay festival brings people together, you know, as well as exciting writers, there are filmmakers, comedians, politicians and musicians to inspire, and entertain you all together. Marvellous – but you've got to get your accommodation sorted out early 'cos B&Bs get booked up fast.

▶ 51

The Brighton festival's great and it's got much bigger over recent years. Er, it's quite international now and got something for all ages and backgrounds. It's also got a huge fringe section too, which makes it cheaper to see things 'cos, you know, the main events can be pricey and sell out very quickly. There's music, comedy, art and instillations, plays, dance, street performance and just mad stuff. The best thing about it though is you get to see great performances in a very fun, chilled out city and then sunbathe on the beach.

12.2

▶ 52

Interviewer: Why do you buy *The Guardian*?

Woman: Well I'm a teacher and there's some very good articles on education and um, then there's jobs in education too, if I ever want to get a new job. And well, it covers world news very thoroughly. I mean, I like the way they report on national and international news ... I think it's the fairest newspaper around.

▶ 53

Woman: Well I think *The Times* is the only paper really worth reading.

Man: Mmmm, but I like to get the *Financial Times* to keep up with what's going on in the money market, ... well it was my job, you see ... er, and at the weekend I like *The Telegraph* for their sports coverage and commentary on the week ...

▶ 54

Man: well, I only ever buy *The Sun*, you see, 'cos it's got a lot of sport reports in there and it's cheaper and smaller than the others – I mean, it's impossible anyway to read one of the bigger ones. It's a bit gossipy but I quite like that.

▶ 55

Woman: Well, I tend to buy the *Daily Mail*, or sometimes the *Daily Express*, because they're good family newspapers ... and because I never finish the broadsheets, you see. I'm very busy working in the shop, our bakery, and looking after my husband and the children. That's enough!

▶ 56

Woman: OK but I like TV, and I just don't see the point of buying a newspaper 'cos I can get all the information I need from the news or my mobile, and I buy my woman's magazine to get all the celeb gossip!

Man: Yeah, but it's important to know what's happening in the world, that's why I get *The Independent*, you know, a couple of times a week or so …

Woman: But I don't have time to read all that stuff and I just want a bit of fun when I read anyway. What's wrong with that?

Man: All right, please yourself …

12.3
▶ 57

John: On the News Today Programme we've got the controller of BBC South Dianne Holme. Di, welcome,

Di: Hello, John.

John: Er, can you give us an idea how important the BBC still is?

Di: Sure, well, the BBC is the principal broadcasting service in Britain and employs more than twenty thousand people, both across the country and abroad.

John: Hmm, that's impressive. Give us a bit of background to the organisation.

Di: Well, as you know, the BBC first started broadcasting in 1922 um, the radio service that is, and the, er, TV network was set up in 1936. The BBC's main centre has remained at the same site in London, at Broadcasting House, since it was built in 1932. Now that it's been upgraded and the new extension's been added, making it the new iconic home of the BBC though some services are now based in Manchester and Glasgow, not forgetting the BBC's regional offices.

John: Yeah, so auntie Beeb's has had a face lift!

Di: Yes, indeed …

John: … and favourites like *EastEnders* and *Dr Who*, will they still be around?

Di: Oh, yes, of course.

John: So tell me a bit more about the BBC World Service. What's the future hold for them after all the cuts?

Di: Well, I personally believe that the World Service is one of the jewels in the BBC's crown. Most people don't realise that it broadcasts 24 hours a day, to over 160 million people and that it reaches over 150 different capital cities on FM radio throughout the world.

John: Important indeed. Now tell me. How independent is the BBC from government interference?

Di: Well, interestingly, BBC Radio was actually the only permitted broadcasting service allowed in the UK until 1967, which is quite a surprise. But everything's changed since then and, as the BBC's paid for by the licence fee, which is about er, £145 per household, it's actually very independent …

John: … and is the future bright?

Di: Yes, I think it's very bright … and the BBC's important to the nation, and we shouldn't forget that it's still the largest international broadcaster in the world.

▶ 58

John: How does the BBC strike a balance between maintaining high-quality programmes and attracting large audiences? We know for a fact that the BBC has been accused of dumbing down and is being pressured to reflect public taste to justify the licence fee …

Di: Well, the BBC has a responsibility to fulfil its charter as well as to entertain licence-paying viewers … and in some circles, it's true, the ratings are now seen as more important than the content or substance.

John: But the problem is, even if you give endless examples of how good the BBC is at dramas, news delivery, factual programmes and so on, its reputation will only be judged as good as the ratings, and this criteria is not always in accordance with quality.

Di: OK, but the real question is, do we want the BBC to promote debate or inform public opinion? … What is our role? Who should we be competing with? Especially with the dramatic changes that are happening every day within the realms of the media and information services. Well, I believe the BBC is here, yes, to not only act as a mirror and reflect public opinion, but it also has a very important role to challenge, inspire and educate people, as stated in its charter. And this is where we should see our role.

13.1
▶ 59

Well, I think that the good thing about schools in the UK is that education is free for all children. In the past, school dinners were free too but now most children must pay for them. It costs about £2 a day for a dinner, so it's still quite cheap. All children must go to school from 5 to 16. In the past teachers could hit children at school, sometimes with a stick. Now they can't hit the children – even if they're very naughty! Classes are quite big with about 27 children in a class on average. All students must take exams at 16. These are called GCSEs. They can leave school after this but many stay at school to take A-Level exams.

14.2
▶ 60

Interviewer: That record was Prokofiev's Suite Number 1 from the ballet, Romeo and Juliet. Now, what's record number 6?

Joe: Well, I'm kind of a child of the 70s and it was a choice between Kate Bush and her song *Wuthering Heights*, you know, based on Emily Brontë's book, or David Bowie. But as he's a contemporary of mine, and one of my favourite singer-songwriters, I've chosen David singing *Heroes*.

Interviewer: Why that track?

Joe: Because it reminds me of my wild rebellious days at art college when anything was possible … for all romantics like me!

Interviewer: Now, we've talked about your love of music and dance and theatre which inspire your work, and your college days, but now we're going to send you off alone with your seven discs. But you're allowed to take one novel, the work of a poet, a film and one luxury item with you. What novel have you chosen to take?

Joe: Well, John, this is really a difficult one … one of my favourite books ever is *White Teeth* by Zadie Smith, and it would remind me of home, but in the end I've chosen the magic world where elves, hobbits and magicians live, you know, *Lord of the Rings* by Tolkien. I started it once but never finished it and I've got all the time in the world to read it there!

Interviewer: And which poet's work would you like to have there with you?

Joe: I'm not usually a big reader of poetry but there are a couple of poets I really love. The first is Carol Ann Duffy, the first female poet laureate – she's from Glasgow like me so I really identify with her.

Interviewer: OK, and who is the second one?

Joe: Benjamin Zephaniah. His poems for adults and children are fantastic … he'll be my final choice as there would be something there for any mood!

Interviewer: And how about a film?

Joe: It has to be something by Danny Boyle… *Slumdog Millionaire*, I think. It's so colourful – and a feel-good movie – some of the others, like *Trainspotting*, are brilliant but a bit darker, maybe.

Interviewer: Excellent choice … and your luxury item?

Joe: Can I take the painting by Millais of Ophelia floating down the river? It's so romantic and dramatic I can transform myself into another world.

Interviewer: You certainly can! So, Joe Davidson, thank you very much for speaking to us today.

Joe: My pleasure.

14.3

▶ 61

I think modern British art displays extraordinary breadth and excitement. The Brit Art movement of the 90s brought us people like Damien Hirst and Tracey Emin and so on, and challenged the status quo of art and artist. I mean, take Tracey Emin's 'My Bed', for example. It engages the viewer in an exploration of her nervous breakdown, as a form of confessional art. Once you accept that she's largely famous for being Tracey, as a critic you either accept the package or you don't. It's similar with Damian Hirst. Take for example, his work 'For the Love of God.' He did none of the stone setting and craftwork but in this work he's kind of summing up art and shameless materialism with a £50 million diamond skull.

On the other hand, you've got Grayson Perry and Banksy. Perry's urns are rendered with great mastery, you know, very intricate Grecian-like urns, but they're images of car-wrecks and mobile-phones … and dark auto-biographical scenes bearing witness to the complex world of his cross-dressing and his female alter ego, Claire. Banksy takes the disguise even further. He is perhaps the most famous, or infamous, artist alive. To some a genius, to others a vandal, as a street artist with a strong political view, he's put 'guerrilla' art in public spaces on the map, like the 'Kissing policeman' or 'Sweeping it under the carpet' and yet his face is still hidden from the public.

I'd say Anish Kapoor is probably the most mainstream artist to come from the 80 and 90s. His spiralling Orbit tower, produced for the 2012 Olympics, is a spectacular collaboration between engineer and sculptor and breaks new ground in blending design and technical mastery of materials, some distance from his earlier work - the blood spattering paint cannon. So, yes British art is strong, challenging and still at the top of its game!

15.1

▶ 62

Raymond: My name's Raymond and I live in an old, thatched cottage in the countryside. It's got three bedrooms and a large kitchen and dining room. I've got a garden and some fruit trees too. Er, my address is … Rose Cottage, Mill Lane, Coleraine, that's C–O–L–E–R–A–I–N–E, in Northern Ireland.

▶ 63

Gareth: Well, we live at 12, Southwood Close in Denby, that's D-E-N-B-Y, in Wales. Megan, my wife, and I moved to this lovely bungalow after my accident on the farm, you see.

Megan: Yeah, we've got two bedrooms and a garden with a shed for Gareth's tools, so we're happy enough.

▶ 64

Holly: Hi, my name's Holly and this is Amos, my husband …

Amos: Yeah, hi. We live in a two-bedroom flat in South London. And we have 2 young boys so it's a bit crowded. Our address is Flat 32, Weston Court, Peckham, that's P–E–C–K–H–A–M, SW99 4AA.

▶ 65

Jamie: Hi, I'm Jamie. I'm a university student and I rent a tiny, one bedroom terraced house in the old part of Edinburgh in Scotland. I live at 4, Mill Street in Edinburgh, and that's spelt, E–D–I–N–B–U–R–G–H, OK?

▶ 66

Interviewer: And where do you live, Lady Searle?

Lady Searle: We're very lucky I suppose. This house has been in our family for over 300 years and it's a very grand country house. Ah, we have nine bedrooms and four living rooms and a library. Our address is … Crestley House, er … that's spelt, C–R–E–S–T–L–E–Y, near the village of Little Beading, that's spelt B–E–A–D–I–N–G, in Kent.

▶ 67

Sirus: Well, we've lived here for 10 years now. Er, it's quite a nice neighbourhood … it's easy to get to work at the clinic, you know …

Aruna: Yeah, we live in a semi-detached house with 4 bedrooms and a large garden. We have 3 children and, oh, my name's Aruna and my husband's Sirus. Our address is, number 16, The Drive, Birmingham B12 7RU

16.3

▶ 68

Over the centuries, the law's gone through many different stages of refinement. In the 18th century, when many cities saw massive growth and even doubled in size, street children, for example, were the outcastes of society, with many living in feral communities, and although children under fourteen couldn't be hanged, they could still be imprisoned or transported to Australia. Life wasn't equal either if a man murdered his wife, he'd be hanged but if a woman murdered her husband, she could be burnt at the stake er, a much worse fate. Hanging wasn't completely banned in Britain until 1969 in fact.

In the 1700s, there were also community punishments for less serious crimes, such as the ducking stool, where women were plunged into rivers for nagging and so on, and men were whipped in the pillory. The Old Bailey records, which are now online, report some very unpleasant examples of rough justice … and indeed transportation to Australia for the tiniest of crimes continued right up to the1860s. Fortunately, the 19th century was also a time of great social reformers, like the MP William Wilberforce, who worked to abolish slavery, and Elizabeth Fry who advocated humane treatment of prisoners, as well as better conditions for the poor – and there were many more. This was the time of the awakening of the idea of civil and human rights, influenced by the French, American and Haitian revolutions …

▶ 69

Presenter:
Professor, what do you think have been the most important changes in law of the last half century?

Prof McAlistair: Well, Clyde, certainly high on the list has to be legislation for equal rights and the strengthening of human rights. The raft of new laws in the mid-70s, for example, promoted the rights of women under the Sex Discrimination Act and Equal Pay Act, er, and BME groups under the Race Relations Act in 1976 and the Disability Discrimination Act of the nineties, they all changed our society. And with the Human Rights Act, promoting the rights of refugees, gay and lesbian couples amongst others, right up to the Equality Act of 2010 protecting the rights of individuals, well, you can see, British society has undergone massive change.

Presenter: And er, what about concerns around the European Union and the law?

Prof McAlistair: Well yeah, I think the EU has had an important effect on us too and we've given many powers to the European Parliament. Both British people and many politicians complain of the impact on our lives, saying we've got little or no control over regulations imposed on us from Brussels.

Presenter: And how have our civil liberties been affected by recent world events?

Prof McAlistair: Well, the civil liberties debate will continue, especially in the aftermath of the July bombings in London in 2005, you remember, when more than 50 people died. Well, the reaction of the Government was to bring in some strict new regulations, holding people longer without trial and house arrest for instance, some of which were challenged and overturned in the law courts.

More recent controversies though are the use of kettling of demonstrators on marches, the use of technology, for example the proliferation of CCTV cameras and the use of electronic tagging on offenders. But what hasn't changed yet is our adversarial court system with prosecutors and defenders, being innocent until proven guilty, and a well established jury system …

17.1

▶ 70

Spring is a very lovely time in Scotland and you can see lots of wildlife. My village is very pretty too and we often go walking in the little wood where you can find red squirrels if you're lucky. And er, in the summer we go up in the hills, and you can often see the deer in the evening drinking from the river, and sometimes our pair of golden eagles flying overhead … Well, near my cottage there are, of course, always rabbits, which are nice for the pot and, em, a fox or two.

▶ 71

This season is often very windy and quite wet in the UK. The trees start to lose their leaves and birds and squirrels are busy in the woods collecting nuts for the winter that's coming. At this time of year the temperature is about 9 degrees. This season is called fall in America but here it's called autumn. Autumn starts on 21st September.

▶ 72

At this time of the year there are many kinds of flowers like roses and tulips in the parks and gardens. The temperature can change from 20 to 28 degrees. Sometimes it can rain a lot in summertime but it's also very warm. People often grow tomatoes, carrots, cucumbers, runner beans and many more vegetables in their gardens as well as flowers. Summer begins on 21st June.

▶ 73

The weather can be very cold in winter with an average temperature of about 4 degrees. In northern England and Scotland a lot more snow falls and it gets dark very early. In the south of England, Wales and Northern Ireland a little snow falls but it can be cold and icy too. Winter starts on 21st December which is the longest night of the year.

▶ 74

This is a beautiful time in the UK. The average temperature is from 10 to 15 degrees and the weather is mild – it can be sunny or rain a lot! The gardens start to grow snowdrops and daffodils and in May the woods are full of bluebells. There is also blossom on lots of trees. Spring begins on 21st March.

17.2

▶ 75

1 I found work much more difficult to find, when I lived in the village. Er, OK, there was always a lot of casual work, farm work or hotel stuff in the summer, but no job security. It's just so much easier getting work in town, especially as you don't have to travel so far, that was another problem for me, getting back and forwards to work from the village – and you get better pay!

▶ 76

2 Well, I work in the city now but I was brought up in the countryside. And one of the problems of living in a village is the cost of housing. It's so expensive to buy a house now, because of all those wealthy people you know, city people, moving in and buying up the properties, that's if you can find a place for sale! Erm, the advantage in the city, of course, is that there are cheaper flats and houses to rent, or buy, or whatever, and you have more choice. But the question is, where do you want to live? Near your family and friends or in a big city full of strangers?

▶ 77

3 Mother: It's such a relaxed way of life in the countryside, you know. The pace of life is so much slower, people have time to talk to each other, and everyone knows each other and there are markets and fetes, sense of community … it's lovely.

Daughter: Yeah, but for young people it's really boring in the country, mum. It'd be much more fun living in town. Erm, you know, town life, it's faster, it makes you feel good. And you've got more choice, like, and it's so much more exciting than living in the middle of nowhere, like here.

▶ 78

4 Well, of course, the environment here's so much healthier than the city. You know, there's more space and you can breathe, do any sport you like, grow your own vegetables and so on. And really, the city, well, it's noisy day and night, and crowded too, and the air's so polluted. I know they have lots of good things too, like parks and community centres and shops and libraries so on, but, personally, I much prefer it here.

18.2

▶ 79

The population of the United Kingdom at the beginning of the 21st century is approximately 61 million. The life expectancy for women in the UK is 82 years but for men it's lower, at about 78. Work in Britain includes jobs in tourism, manufacturing, and IT. Also very important are business, banking, and local government. There are also lots of jobs in call centres and shops. The NHS is the biggest employer though.

Generally, healthcare is much improved but problems include obesity, heart disease, and cancer. People also have problems related to alcohol and smoking. There's more choice of food but many people still have unhealthy diets and eat too much fat, sugar and carbohydrates, although fresh and organic food is becoming more popular.

People's leisure time activities still include TV and film, but computer entertainment and DVDs have become much more common. Traditional activities such as dancing, music, pubs and restaurants are still popular too.

As for world news, the century started with wars in Afghanistan and Iraq. Britain continues to support international action to slow down climate change. Politicians still debate the role of Britain in the world. On the home news front, the huge crash in world markets continues to affect the economy and the gap between rich and poor continues to widen.